One World
MULTICULTURAL
Projects & Activities

Susan Blackaby

Troll Associates

ISBN: 0-8167-2598-5

Printed in the United States of America.

10 9 8 7 6 5 4 3

Contents

One World:
Multicultural
Projects & Activities
Meeting the Needs of Today's Students

A primary goal of education is to provide students with the tools that will enable them independently to develop perception and evaluate information, so that they may successfully sort out the complexities of their environment and gain an understanding of their roles and responsibilities. Developing a sense of self and of one's relationship to others is a crucial part of this process, but it has traditionally been overlooked or minimized in favor of group identity and an emphasis on conformity. Educators have found, however, that the wide-ranging demographics reflected in the classroom population must be recognized and supported; understanding must be fostered; individuality must be validated.

Who are your students? Which child speaks more than one language? Which child lives with a group of extended family members? Which child works in the family business? Which child is getting support—or pressure—from home to excel? Is that passive learner quiet out of respect or out of self-consciousness? Efforts to answer these and similar questions in the context of today's classroom reveal culturally derived differences in students' behavior, expectations, and orientations. It is not enough to acknowledge these differences; they must be clarified, explored, and understood. And they must be celebrated.

One World: Multicultural Projects & Activities provides students with the opportunity for such a celebration. This book encourages examination of the beliefs, values, knowledge, and customs that each individual brings to the creation of the whole—the cooperative group, the class, the school, the city, the state, the nation —and provides opportunities that will support the development of empathy and self-appreciation. When students learn to appreciate one another's individuality, they will also develop a strong, positive sense of self that is the most critical factor in achievement.

One World:
Multicultural
Projects & Activities
Meeting the Needs of Today's Teachers

The following components are provided for teacher and student use.

Opening Project Pages The opening project pages in this book (pages 8–9) will help students discover some of the many answers to the question "Who am I?" by fostering an awareness of heritage, traditions, customs, and culture. Students are required to consult a wide range of resource materials in exploring their individuality, and parents and family members are encouraged to participate. Students present their findings to classmates in lively, colorful ways.

Background Information Introductions to cultures provide background information to give teachers a brief overview of events, circumstances, and traditions that influence cultural conventions.

Project Pages Project pages present a series of cooperative activities. Projects provide a context for learning about each culture and offer interesting ways to gather and present information that will prepare them for the ideas they will encounter in the reading selections. Students work together and share their findings.

Reading Selections For each culture, reading selections from folk tales, history/oral history, and contemporary fiction have been reviewed to provide teachers with a starting point. Selections have been chosen for their accuracy, authenticity, literary merit, availability, and variety, and represent many different voices, experiences, and views. Selections within each culture and genre are suitable for a wide range of elementary students' abilities and interests; there is something for every learner in grades K through 6. Each book review includes information about the author and illustrator, as well as a classroom discussion question, which is highlighted on the page by a globe. These books can be read aloud to students or placed in a special classroom reading center for independent or group projects.

Moving Beyond the Books The activities on these pages are derived from but not confined to reading selections. They may be assigned to students for cooperative learning or independent enrichment. Reading, writing, speaking and listening, research, and creative skills are applied as students explore point of view, historical perspective, role-playing, current events, creative writing, and art.

One World:
Multicultural
Projects & Activities
Meeting the Needs of Today's Curriculum

Educators have determined that slotting multicultural lessons into existing programs or focusing on multicultural topics only in conjunction with special events or holidays lacks the depth of study necessary to meet goals of understanding. Building a multicultural curriculum from the ground up is an educational innovation that is yet to be realized on a nationwide scale. But, working toward that goal, teachers are looking for ways to incorporate multicultural awareness into their daily lesson plans.

One World: Multicultural Projects & Activities can be used as a framework that will support all aspects of the curriculum. The open-ended character of the projects makes them excellent ''jumping-off points'' for focusing on multicultural topics within particular disciplines, and the new facts and intriguing ideas students will discover in doing their projects can be applied in follow-up discussions, problem solving, and critical thinking. Projects and activities in which students practice basic skills to solve problems can be tailored to fit a variety of academic subjects. Reading selections can be chosen and applied to a range of topics that may be introduced to the entire group working together, used by teams of students working cooperatively, or explored by individuals working independently.

One World: Multicultural Projects & Activities provides teachers with enough material to design a multiculturally oriented lesson plan that can last throughout the school year. The ideas and information presented in the book can be supplemented in classroom talks with outside agencies, parents, and school and local librarians to create a comprehensive course of study. A multicultural curriculum will enrich and enhance the lives of students, and the benefits the students derive will ultimately benefit all of society.

Your Own Roots

Branch Out

Have your family help you design a family tree. How many generations can you identify? (Include the generation that you are in.) How many different countries do your ancestors come from? Write your answers to these questions underneath your family tree.

Folks' Tales

Where did your grandparents or great-grandparents or even great-great-grandparents come from? Find a folk tale from a country or region where your ancestors lived. Practice retelling it. Share it with the class.

Your Own Flag

Choose up to four countries that you can identify in your ancestry. With a pencil, divide a large sheet of paper into as many sections as you have countries. Draw the flag of each country in a section of the sheet. You may want to draw flags on the other side, displaying the states or provinces where your parents were born, the countries, provinces, or states you have lived in, and so on. Attach the finished flag to a stick and display it in the classroom. You and your friends may want to have a flag parade!

Read All About It

Find out or estimate the year a grandparent, great-grandparent, or great-great-grandparent was born. Find out an important event from that year. If possible, find out what was happening in the country or city where the person was born. Write about the event as a news story, complete with a headline. Display your front-page news on a bulletin board.

State Statements

Find out the state slogans or national mottoes that represent your family background. Write the slogans on strips of paper or on adding machine tape and display them in the classroom.

8

Pinpoint Your Heritage

Get together with your classmates and locate your ancestors' birthplaces on a world map. Mark the locations with map pins. Use green pins for parents, yellow pins for grandparents, red pins for great-grandparents, and blue pins for great-great-grandparents.

Me Oh My

Design a personalized license plate that says—and shows—something about the *real* you. Display your plate on a bulletin board.

Blue Ribbon Name Tag

Make a name tag for yourself. Your tag may include where your name came from, including the origin of your last name or the person you are named after. Attach ribbons to your tag and label them with the name of the state or country where each of your parents and grandparents was born. Use different colors of ribbon for parents and grandparents.

Welcome to My World

Immediate families and extended families often have their own unique way of communicating that may include special stories, poems, songs, lullabies, sayings, vocabulary, or names for objects. Give an oral report in which you share "oral traditions" of your family with the rest of the class. You may focus on one of the ideas listed above. Or you may want to describe a family tradition and explain its origins.

Sing Along

Choose one of the countries that your ancestors came from. Learn the national anthem or a traditional song from that country and teach it to the class.

Talk of the Town

What languages did your ancestors speak? Look up some of the words they used and learn to pronounce them. Use index cards to make foreign-language labels for items around the classroom. Learn to introduce yourself in the language.

Family Forum

Invite parents and other immediate and extended family members to participate in a family forum, so that they can see your work on this project. Plan a program to present some of the folk tales and stories, share your displays, sing your songs, and share your discoveries.

Exploring African-American Culture

In this section, students explore the African continent to get an overview of its natural, political, and social history; they are introduced to folk tales from Africa as well as traditional African-American folklore tied to the American South; they focus on biographical and autobiographical accounts of African Americans, both prominent and ordinary citizens, throughout U.S. history; and they are exposed to contemporary African-American poetry and fiction that reflect a broad range of experience and points of view.

The ancestors of most African Americans came from the many populations and cultures located in West Africa. More than a hundred languages were spoken in the region, and empires flourished for centuries before colonies were established on American soil. It is important for students to realize that the people sold into slavery were mothers, fathers, teachers, healers, warriors, royalty, farmers, artists, children—members of established communities.

Many of the genetic, linguistic, and cultural distinctions that existed among Africans brought to the United States were dissolved by over two centuries of slavery, and with them the continuity of ancestral traditions and ties. Having lost the immediacy of their heritage, African Americans developed new customs that were independent of patterns established by Americans of European ancestry.

Social structures that free people took for granted were forbidden to slaves, who often fraternized in secret. Sophisticated secret slave communities were led by generous, equitable, and charismatic people who were able to forge hope out of hardship and faith out of fear. Within these communities, family relationships were established, moral codes were defined, and spiritual pathways were followed. African-American spiritual communities formed around a hybrid religion that combined elements of West African beliefs with Christianity. A society began to take shape, and with it, an environment in which imagination and expression could take flight.

Products of the new culture flourish today in many areas including the fine and performing arts. American popular music evolved from spirituals, the blues, and jazz; elements of choreography unique to a variety of American dance styles were designed and developed by African-American dancers. In addition, African Americans developed a rich store of fables and folk tales even though for the majority it was illegal to learn to read and write. Elaborate narratives derived from African oral traditions were passed from generation to generation. African-American folk tales characteristically feature plots in which one character overcomes another more powerful character by means of quick wit and ingenuity, embodying the spirit and struggle of the African-American slave.

Out of or in spite of a legacy of suffering and separation, African Americans have developed a rich, singular culture. African-American contributions are reflected in all levels and aspects of American society.

PROJECT PAGE

Overview of the African Continent

Get together with your group. Choose a contemporary African country to be your focus for the following activities.

Nature

Make a map of your focus country that shows some of the most important natural resources, geographical features, and areas where certain animals and plants thrive.

Politics

What is the current form of government in your focus country? What forms of government have dominated it in the past? Who are the best-known rulers in your country's history? What major factors have influenced your focus country, including colonial rule and shifting populations?

Society

Who lives in your focus country? What different ethnic groups are there? What is the official language? What other languages are spoken? What kinds of social systems exist in your focus country, including community structures, family structure, education?

Culture

Find out how people in your focus country express themselves through art, literature, crafts, textiles, music, dance, drama, celebration. Let members of your group choose different forms of expression to explore and prepare presentations for the class. Possibilities include telling a folk tale, reading a poem, sewing a traditional costume, copying a characteristic design onto fabric or paper, creating pieces of jewelry to model or display.

Reporting

Get together with the other groups and fit your map pieces together to form a bulletin-board display of the African continent. Have your group share the information it collected by giving an oral report that includes your Cultural History presentation. Discuss how your focus country compares with other African nations, including similarities and interdependence.

Turtle Knows Your Name

Retold and illustrated by Ashley Bryan
Atheneum, 1989

Turtle Knows Your Name is an adaptation of a West Indian tale. It is
the story of a little boy with a long name that is easy to pronounce but
not so easy to remember. Patiently, the boy's grandmother teaches
him his name, and when he gets it right, they celebrate with a name
dance on the beach. Turtle, who has gathered names of all the children
since before Granny was a child, swims over the watch and then dives
deep to spell out the name in shells: UPSILIMANA TUMPALERADO.
Though the boy now knows his name, no one else can remember it,
and the animals don't care what it is—except for one old turtle. And,
as it turns out, the same holds true for Granny's name.

The cadence of Bryan's language is always on the verge of song, with
intermittent echoes of a drum beat in the background. The paintings
share this movement, and the tropical colors Bryan uses evoke the
warm, merry relationship among the characters.

Ashley Bryan is a native of New York City. For years he taught art at
Dartmouth College, but he has moved to Maine, where he writes and
paints full time.

*How do you think Upsilimana Tumpalerado feels
about people not being able to remember his
name? How would you feel? Have you ever been
called by a nickname you didn't like? Have you
ever been called by the wrong name? How did
you feel?*

Mother Crocodile

By Birago Diop
Translated and adapted by Rosa Guy
Illustrated by John Steptoe
Delacorte, 1981

Mother Crocodile is a traditional tale from Senegal that emphasizes the importance of heeding the lessons of one's elders. As the little crocodiles in this story learn, wisdom may have many disguises in the rambling and seemingly pointless tales of the past. The little crocodiles take Mother Crocodile's stories to heart just in time to save themselves from disaster. Readers are also introduced to the origins of animal traits and talents—rabbits' ears, parrots' mimicry, monkeys' gossip, hyenas' behavior—and to the interdependence of animals, people, and the environment.

The character of Mother Crocodile is juxtaposed with that of Uncle Amadou, the storyteller. Amadou tells the story of Mother Crocodile, who is telling the stories to the little crocodiles. This device evokes the cyclical aspect of nature and provides another lesson for students to explore: History repeats itself . . . all the more reason to listen carefully to one's elders.

John Steptoe's illustrations are reminiscent of the fabric painting of Senegal.

Birago Diop is a native of Senegal. His storyteller, Amadou Koumba, was the household storyteller in Diop's grandmother's house. Diop has translated many of Amadou Koumba's bedtime stories into French, the official language of Senegal.

Rosa Guy met Diop on a trip to Senegal and decided to translate his tales from French into English so that English-speaking children would be able to enjoy the beauty and richness of Senegalese folklore.

What do you think the little crocodiles will do the next time Mother Crocodile begins to tell them a story?

Why Mosquitoes Buzz in People's Ears

By Verna Aardema
Pictures by Leo and Diane Dillon
Dial, 1975

An iguana who does not want to be pestered by a mosquito's nonsense plugs up his ears with sticks and goes on his way. His subsequent inability to hear sets off a series of reactions that ultimately causes the accidental death of an owlet. As a result, Mother Owl becomes so distraught that she cannot bring herself to wake the sun, and the jungle is plunged into confusion. The lion, the king of the jungle, hears everyone's version of the events, revealing misunderstandings galore. He is able to solve the problem to everyone's satisfaction, including that of Mother Owl, who hoots for the rising of the sun. Meanwhile, the mosquito, recognized as the culprit, escapes the animals' judgement, but her guilty conscience causes her to ask people if the animals are still mad, an annoying habit that persists to this day.

Onomatopoeia and refraining text set up a distinctive, musical rhythm that gives life and clarity to the story. Bright, large-scale illustrations by Leo and Diane Dillon helped to earn this book the 1976 Caldecott Medal for the Most Distinguished Picture Book for Children.

Verna Aardema was born in New Era, Michigan, and educated at Michigan State University. She lives in Muskegon, Michigan. Ms. Aardema is a celebrated storyteller and is the author of **Who's in Rabbit's House?**, an ALA Notable Children's Book.

How would this tale have been different if the iguana had been more tolerant of the mosquito's story?

The Knee-High Man and Other Tales

By Julius Lester

Illustrated by Ralph Pinto

Dial, 1972

Julius Lester learned to appreciate the pure pleasure of storytelling by listening to his father. Traditional tales found in African-American culture—including historical tales, fables, and parables—have been told and retold for generations. As a college student, Lester began collecting these animal tales in their myriad versions and exploring a rich aspect of his heritage. Six charming animal tales are presented here, accompanied by detailed illustrations by Ralph Pinto.

The People Could Fly: American Black Folktales

Told by Virginia Hamilton

Illustrated by Leo and Diane Dillon

Knopf, 1985

Virginia Hamilton's collection of tales includes animal tales, fanciful stories, legends of the supernatural, and true accounts of African-American slaves' escapes to the North. Hamilton provides background information for every story, explaining their subtleties and tracing their origins. She also provides a glossary of Gullah English words and phrases included in the stories.

Illustrations by Leo and Diane Dillon highlight the text, giving these fine old stories a new look. The Dillons received the Caldecott Medal in 1976 for **Why Mosquitoes Buzz in People's Ears** and in 1977 for **Ashanti to Zulu.**

Virginia Hamilton is a distinguished author of children's fiction. Her work has won such awards as the Newbery Medal, the Boston Globe–Horn Book Award, the National Book Award, the Coretta Scott King Award, and the Edgar Allan Poe Award. Hamilton was educated at Antioch College and Ohio State University, with further study at the New School for Social Research. She is married to the poet Arnold Adoff.

How did African Americans use the characteristics of animals to depict human personality traits in their folklore?

African-American Folk Tales

Retelling Tales

Choose a traditional folk tale from the South. Read it and practice telling it several times before presenting it to the class. You do not need to memorize the tale word-for-word. Keep in mind the sequence of events and then tell the story in your own words, adding details and descriptions that will help set the scene.

Show Buzz-ness

Get together with your group and act out **Why Mosquitoes Buzz in People's Ears.** First rewrite the story in the form of a play. Then decide who will play each role. You may wish to make a mask for each character and create some simple props. Rehearse the play a few times before performing it for the rest of the class.

The Tale of the Bear

Write an original animal folk tale like those in **The Knee-High Man and Other Tales** and in **The People Could Fly: American Black Folktales.** Include a variety of animals and plenty of dialogue in your story. Use descriptive words to set the scene. You may wish to use one of the following situations to get started:

- Your main character has to find a way to cross safely through a rival's berry bushes in order to take a shortcut home.
- Your main character is caught in a trap and tricks a rival into setting him free.
- Your main character convinces a rival to trade a bushel of carrots for all the water in the river.

Why Mosquitoes Buzz in People's Ears
Verna Aardema
The Knee-High Man and Other Tales
Julius Lester
The People Could Fly: American Black Folktales
Virginia Hamilton

John Henry: An American Legend

Story and pictures by Ezra Jack Keats
Pantheon, 1965

John Henry is a larger-than-life figure who embodies the spirit of America. In a famous legend, John Henry uses a hammer and pick to race a steam-powered drill. This story has been traced to miners drilling the Big Bend tunnel on the Chesapeake & Ohio Railroad in the 1870s and may have some basis in fact. John Henry is the subject of numerous songs and stories. This work by Ezra Jack Keats is poetic and emotionally charged. Keats's clarity of language coupled with his dynamic illustrations evoke the pure power of this legendary African-American man.

Ezra Jack Keats spent most of his life in New York. He began his artistic career as a muralist before illustrating children's books. He won the 1963 Caldecott Medal for **The Snowy Day.** Other noteworthy titles include **Whistle for Willie, God Is in the Mountain, Jennie's Hat,** and **Peter's Chair.** Keats also designed holiday cards for UNICEF.

John Henry is a legend, a story that has been passed down from generation to generation. Characteristics of a legendary figure are often exaggerated over time, as more and more people retell the story. Which details in the story of John Henry do you think are true? Which might be exaggerations? Give reasons for your answers.

Young Frederick Douglass: Fight for Freedom

By Laurence Santrey

Illustrated by Bert Dodson

Troll Associates, 1983

This biography highlights events in the life of Frederick Douglass, focusing on his childhood and touching on many of his accomplishments as a freedman. It offers a grim account of the brutality and injustice of his life as a slave on a Southern plantation, enabling students to empathize with the hardships of a child their own age. The critical importance of a slave's learning to read is apparent; reading played a key role in Douglass's escape to freedom. The book also chronicles the many contributions Douglass made and the risks he took as an adult in the African-American struggle for freedom, including publishing an abolitionist newspaper and speaking out against slavery with eloquence and urgency. During the Civil War, Douglass persuaded President Lincoln to allow black soldiers to fight for the Union. After the war and Emancipation, Douglass continued to speak out, advocating civil rights for all people.

Laurence Santrey grew up in St. Louis, Missouri. His books for young readers include numerous biographies as well as nonfiction on a variety of topics. He lives with his family in Abilene, Kansas.

Bert Dodson's rich illustrations bring alive the people and situations Frederick Douglass encounters on his journey to freedom.

How was learning to read a key factor in changing Douglass's life? How did Mrs. Betsey Baily and Mrs. Auld influence and change the course of Douglass's life?

Harriet Tubman: The Road to Freedom

By Rae Bains
Illustrated by Larry Johnson
Troll Associates, 1982

This biography of Harriet Tubman recounts her childhood as a slave on a Maryland plantation, her escape on the Underground Railroad, and her life as a legendary conductor who helped hundreds find their way to freedom. Tubman suffered from frequent illness and from injury at the hands of slave holders. She derived her considerable inner strength from her family, her faith, and the stories of slaves who fought for freedom. She believed that God would not abandon her people, and that belief kept her dream of freedom alive.

Rae Bains grew up in Dayton, Ohio. She is a writer and teacher with a special interest in civil rights and social justice. In addition to biographies, Bains has published several articles about Martin Luther King, Jr.

Larry Johnson brings Harriet Tubman's story alive with his expressive pen and ink drawings.

What do you most admire about Harriet Tubman?

The Black Americans: A History in Their Own Words

Edited by Milton Meltzer
Crowell, 1984

The Black Americans gives upper-grade readers a diverse array of African-American thoughts, opinions, ideas, experiences, history, and study. Culling letters, journals, public records, autobiographies, newspaper and magazine articles, transcripts, and reports, Meltzer has compiled material dating from 1619 onward, chronicling over 350 years of hardship and achievement by black men, women, and children. Slaves and former slaves, freedmen, insurrectionists, abolitionists, poets, soldiers, writers, artists, educators, journalists, preachers, and politicians describe their experiences and give voice to history. Included in this anthology are the moving words of Sojourner Truth, Frederick Douglass, Harriet Tubman, Martin Luther King, Jr., Maya Angelou, and Langston Hughes. An editorial note introduces each author, establishing a context. Sources are provided at the end of each entry.

Milton Meltzer is a biographer and historian. He has written over seventy books for young people and adults on a wide range of subjects and has edited and written for books, magazines, newspapers, radio, and film. He has had several nominations for the National Book Award and has won numerous other awards, including ALA awards.

How do firsthand accounts make history come alive?

African-American History/Oral History

Down to Size

Think about the qualities that make a person seem larger than life. Legends are often based on facts that have been stretched and exaggerated. John Henry may have been a real person who was greatly respected and admired by those who worked with him on the railroad. Pretend that you worked with John Henry. Tell what he was like and describe what happened in the real-life story.

A Life of Its Own

Get together with a small group. Turn an original story, a historical event, or a newspaper story into a legend. Have one person write the real-life story. Have another student in the group read the story and rewrite it, adding details that will make the story more interesting. Then pass along the story to another student to read and rewrite. Continue until the story has been rewritten three or four times. Present each version in order to the class.

   Discuss how the details change and descriptions grow as the legend takes shape.

A Different Point of View

In 1838, Frederick Douglass boarded a crowded train in Baltimore. He was disguised as a sailor and carried the free papers of a friend. Pretend that you are a conductor on the train. You feel certain that Douglass is a slave making his escape to the North, but you do not study his papers closely or question his freedom to travel. Describe the scene. Tell what you are thinking. Why don't you turn him in? What are your feelings as you look into Douglass's eyes?

John Henry: An American Legend
Ezra Jack Keats
Young Frederick Douglass: Fight for Freedom
Laurence Santrey

Jambo Means Hello:
Swahili Alphabet Book

By Muriel Feelings
Pictures by Tom Feelings
Dial, 1974

This book presents Swahili words and their pronunciations while also providing insights into the traditions, life-styles, conventions, etiquette, art forms, and environments of speakers of Swahili. Detailed illustrations by Tom Feelings enhance the information in the text. In spite of its brevity and, at first glance, simplicity, **Jambo Means Hello** is a thought-provoking introduction to African life.

Muriel Feelings was born in Philadelphia and educated in California. She taught in East Africa for two years and now resides in Philadelphia, where she is active in African-American community organizations. **Moja Means One: Swahili Counting Book** was a Caldecott Honor Book in 1974.

Well-known artist and illustrator Tom Feelings was born in Brooklyn and attended the School of Visual Arts. He has lived in Ghana and has traveled extensively in East Africa.

Hodi? (You may wish to surprise your students with this Swahili question from the book. The correct response is *Karibu*.)

Under the Sunday Tree

Poems by Eloise Greenfield
Paintings by Amos Ferguson
Harper, 1988

This collection of poems captures the spirit of the Bahamas, on both paper and canvas. Eloise Greenfield's words echo the pulse and rhythm of daily life, while Amos Ferguson's vibrant colors highlight the setting.

What about the poems and illustrations in Under the Sunday Tree *would make you want to visit the Bahamas?*

Nathaniel Talking

By Eloise Greenfield
Illustrated by Jan Spivey Gilchrist
Black Butterfly, 1988

Nine-year-old Nathaniel B. Free meets the world head-on in this collection of rap and rhyme. Each entry reflects Nathaniel's lively attitude and attempts to explain the events and circumstances that comprise his world. Pencil drawings by Jan Spivey Gilchrist evoke the warmth and personality of this jazzy little character.

Eloise Greenfield has been an artist-in-education for the Washington, D.C., Commission on the Arts and Humanities, sharing her gift for creative writing with students. She has received numerous awards for her fiction, biography, and poetry, which are aimed at providing "nourishing literature for children."

If you could spend the afternoon with Nathaniel B. Free, what would you do together?

Jafta
Jafta's Father
Jafta and the Wedding

Stories by Hugh Lewin
Pictures by Lisa Kopper
Carolrhoda Books, 1983

These three books by Hugh Lewin feature Jafta, a young black South African boy.

In **Jafta,** students are introduced to the many facets of Jafta's personality. Jafta's moods, traits, dreams, and desires are compared to characteristics of African animals in a series of similes.

In **Jafta's Father,** Jafta compares his father's strength and stature to the trees in his village and recalls a fort-building project that the two of them completed together. Jafta's father is living and working in the city, and Jafta keenly feels the separation. Jafta's friend teases him and says his father isn't coming back, but his mother assures him that his father will return in the spring, and Jafta holds onto that hope.

In **Jafta and the Wedding,** Jafta describes the week of festivities leading up to his sister Nomsa's wedding. Day by day, Jafta tells about the preparations and wedding customs. Jafta and his friends are caught up in the excitement as the day approaches, and everyone in the village participates in the joyous celebration.

Hugh Lewin was born in South Africa and now resides in Zimbabwe. He is the author of a work of adult nonfiction entitled **Bandiet: Seven Years in a South African Prison,** which describes his incarceration for his opposition to apartheid. Upon his release, Lewin moved to England and started a family. His books emerged from his desire to acquaint his young daughters with his South African childhood and with their own roots.

Lisa Kopper has collaborated with Lewin on all of the books about Jafta. Her illustrations convey the joy of Jafta's lively character and lend insight into South African life-styles, traditions, and customs.

What do you think you would enjoy most about visiting Jafta and his family?

Justin and the Best Biscuits in the World

By Mildred Pitts Walter
Alfred A. Knopf, 1986

In **Justin and the Best Biscuits in the World,** ten-year-old Justin is invited by his cowboy grandfather to visit Grandpa's ranch. While there, Justin learns about some famous black cowboys in history—Jessie Stahl and Deadwood Dick—and the work they did training broncos, branding calves, and driving cattle. In his room at the ranch, Justin reads a book about his great-great-grandfather who brought the family from Tennessee into Missouri, fifteen years after the slaves were freed.

Justin and his grandfather enjoy a day at a festival, complete with rodeo, games, and contests. Grandpa wins first prize in the Best Biscuits in the World contest, and, for the first time in his life, Justin wants to learn to bake. At the end of his visit, Justin returns to his family with a new view of black cowboys in history and of men and women's responsibilities today.

Justin and the Best Biscuits in the World received the Coretta Scott King Award.

Mildred Pitts Walter makes her home in Denver, Colorado, though she travels extensively as an educational consultant promoting the accessibility of African-American culture.

In what ways did Justin behave differently with his mother and sisters after his trip to Grandpa's ranch? What were the reasons for the change?

African-American Contemporary Fiction

Poem and Palette

The poems and paintings in **Under the Sunday Tree** give a view of life in the Bahamas. When you think of where you live or you look at the land around you, what colors come to mind? Write a poem that captures the sights, smells, noises, and feelings of your everyday world. Illustrate your poem, using the colors of home.

Me Talking

Get together with a group and write some rap music pieces like those in **Nathaniel Talking.** Perform your piece for your class. You may write one long piece about an issue that is important to you. Or you may want to write several short pieces that can be put together in a program. For example, you might write several short pieces to describe your day: getting up in the morning; going to school; playing ball; having supper, doing chores, finishing homework; resting for tomorrow.

Dear Father, Dear Jafta

Jafta's father is away from home, working in the city. Write a letter from Jafta to his father. Tell about all of the things going on in the village. Describe what you are up to while he is away. Draw him a picture of yourself playing with your friends or helping your mother.

If you wish, you may send Jafta a reply from his father. Tell how much you miss Jafta and how different the city is from the village. Design a stamp to go on the envelope. Post your letters, pictures, and stamp designs on a bulletin board in the classroom.

Under the Sunday Tree
Nathaniel Talking
Eloise Greenfield
Jafta's Father
Hugh Lewin

Exploring Native-American Cultures

In this section, students explore the life-styles of individual Native-American groups to discover the cultural and environmental distinctions from one group to another; they study Native-American folklore; they gain insight into Native-American cultural and political history through firsthand accounts and ethnography; they gain an understanding of Native Americans' efforts to preserve their traditions, images, beliefs, and values through contemporary fiction and poetry.

Essential to any study of Native Americans is realizing the diversity and cultural sophistication of the Native-American population. When the first Europeans arrived, hundreds of tribes were spread across the North American continent. All Native-American tribes established practices that reflected a keen understanding of the environment. Interaction among the various tribes included cooperation and trade, expansion and invasion, warfare and strife. Although these groups may have honored reciprocal agreements and interacted in elaborate trade networks, social unity among the groups has been a relatively recent development as populations of individual tribes have decreased or disappeared and tribes within geographical regions have been consolidated. Each tribe has its own characteristics, language or dialect, customs, traditions, values, codes, and beliefs that comprise its identity; similarities and differences from one tribe to another are important to acknowledge and explore.

Native-American groups have traditionally been classified into the following geocultural divisions: Arctic, Subarctic, Northwest Coast, Woodlands, Plains, California, Basin-Plateau, and Southwest. These groups' traditional geographical classifications are as follows. *Arctic groups* (Inuit): along the Northern coastline of North America, from the Bering Sea to Greenland. *Subarctic groups* (e.g. Chippewa or Ojibwa, Yellowknife, Chipewyan): across most of Canada. *Northwest Coast groups* (e.g. Chinook, Kwakiutl, Haida, Nootka): from southern Alaska to northern California. *Woodlands groups:* across the eastern part of the United States from the Atlantic Ocean to the Mississippi River and the Great Lakes; within this region, there are Northeast groups (e.g. Iroquois, Delaware, Susquehanna) and Southeast groups (e.g. Seminole, Choctaw, Cherokee). *Plains groups* (e.g. Sioux, Blackfeet, Comanche, Cheyenne): in the middle of North America, from north of the U.S./Canada border to Texas, bordered on the west by the Rocky Mountains and on the east by the Mississippi River. *California groups* (e.g. Pomo, Hupa, Yokut): in the area that is now the state of California. *Basin-Plateau groups* (e.g. Paiute, Nez Perce, Shoshone): from above the U.S./Canada border through the Rocky Mountain plateau to the Southwest and California. *Southwest groups* (e.g. Navajo, Papago, Pueblo): in Arizona, New Mexico, parts of Colorado, and Utah.

The survival of the ways of life that are unique to each tribe depends on the understanding and cooperation of all American people. Preserving Native-American languages and dialects, collecting folklore, recording history, celebrating rites, and teaching skills and techniques require extraordinary effort and commitment.

Artic:Inuit

NW coast   Sioux, Cheyenne

SE: Seminole, Cherokee

NE   Iroquois

SW   Navaho
         Pueblo

Native Americans Yesterday and Today

Get together with your group. Choose a Native American tribe to be your focus. Then choose one of the following activities.

Act It Out

Write a play that shows ancestors of the people in your focus tribe at work. What are the traditional roles for each member of the group? What is the tribe's life-style? Make simple props, costumes, and backgrounds to help you set the scene.

Tribal Mural

Paint a mural that shows the daily life of your focus tribe's ancestors. How was food collected and prepared? What did the village look like? Did people live in permanent dwellings, or did they move from one camp to another? You may wish to paint two separate murals to show how village life changed from summer to winter.

Tribal Time Line

Make a time line showing the history of your focus tribe, up to and including the present day. Highlight major figures in tribal life and the events that have affected the people of your tribe.

Reporting

Have your group make its presentation to the rest of the class. Discuss similarities and differences you observe among the tribes.

Mouse Woman and the Vanished Princesses

By Christie Harris

Drawings by Douglas Tait

Atheneum, 1976

Mouse Woman is a familiar figure in Northwest Native-American lore. She is known for her primness, her goodness, and her intervention in the mischief and trickery of other supernatural beings, known as narnauks. In this collection of original stories, princesses of the Northwest tribes—prized for their beauty, influence, wealth, and challenging inaccessibility—are lured from their families by the cunning of narnauks. Each is rescued from her predicament by the Mouse Woman, who appears as a white mouse and as a tiny, grandmotherly character—but Mouse Woman must first be shown the respect she is due, and her quirky need to pick into a fleecy nest a bit of wool from an ear ornament or a shawl must be indulged.

Christie Harris has pursued her writing about Western Canadian history and Native Americans of the Northwest Coast throughout the course of her career as a teacher in British Columbia. Titles include **Once upon a Totem, West with the White Chiefs,** and **Raven's Cry.** This third title received the Book of the Year medal from the Canadian Association of Children's Librarians.

Would Mouse Woman truly abandon a rude and ungrateful princess?

Quillworker: A Cheyenne Legend

Written and Adapted by Terri Cohlene
Illustrated by Charles Reasoner
Watermill Press, 1990

Quillworker: A Cheyenne Legend tells the story of a Cheyenne girl with a special gift for creating quillwork designs. Her skill and artistry are unsurpassed even by the most accomplished women in the tribe. In dreams, Quillworker is directed to create seven sets of warrior's garments. She crafts each one meticulously with her original designs. When she is finished, she takes the clothing on a seven-day journey from her people, where seven brothers are waiting for her to be their sister, just as her dreams foretold. There, Quillworker learns that the youngest brother has summoned her through his powers. Quillworker's peaceful life with the brothers is disrupted by Buffalo Calf, Buffalo Cow, and Buffalo Bull; each one in turn demands that Quillworker come make them beautiful and threatens the brothers' lives when they refuse to give her up. The youngest brother uses his power to effect an escape, transporting the group to the sky to become the first stars—the Big Dipper and the North Star—and night after night Quillworker's designs glow in the sky.

Following the story is an ethnographic overview of the Cheyenne, with maps and photographs, along with a time line and glossary of terms used in the story. Examples of quillwork and Cheyenne pictographs are also included.

Charles Reasoner's highly stylized illustrations capture the magic of the story. Students might like to try creating versions of his illuminated manuscript designs in their own writings.

Charles Reasoner is a Seattle-based free-lance artist who began his career in design and advertising. After twelve years he switched to illustrating children's books full time, and he has worked on over one hundred titles. His research for the watercolors in **Quillworker: A Cheyenne Legend** took him on a two-year journey throughout North America, searching for Cheyenne designs and symbols that would add meaning to the text.

Imagine that you were Quillworker's mother. If you had known what was going to happen to your daughter, would you have prevented her from going to the brothers?

The Sound of Flutes and Other Indian Legends

Transcribed and edited by Richard Erdoes
Pictures by Paul Goble
Pantheon, 1976

Richard Erdoes collected the stories in **The Sound of Flutes and Other Indian Legends** over twenty-five years of listening to his friends: Henry Crow Dog, Strange Owl, He Dog, Lame Deer, Jenny Leading Cloud, Leonard Crow Dog, Eagle Elk, Good White Buffalo, Jake Herman, Spotted Elk, Rachel Strange Owl, George Eagle Elk. All of the legends come from the traditions of the Plains Indians: Sioux, Cheyenne, Gros Ventre, Crow. The transcriptions capture the distinctive voices and styles of the storytellers, from informal, brief, humorous accounts to formal, embellished narratives. Erdoes has also included the introductory and editorial comments sprinkled throughout the stories by the storytellers, providing a unique historical and cultural context for the legends and insight into the personal histories of the tellers.

Richard Erdoes is an artist, photographer, and writer who divides his time between New York City and Santa Fe. He first made contact with Southwest Native Americans while on a painting assignment to depict the scenery, people, and life of the Plains. Erdoes is the author of comprehensive accounts of Native-American life and is a strong supporter of the Indian Civil Rights Movement.

Which of the Native Americans telling these stories would you most like to meet and listen to in person? Explain your reasons.

Ladder to the Sky

Retold by Barbara Juster Esbensen
Illustrated by Helen K. Davie
Little, Brown, 1989

Ladder to the Sky is an Ojibwa (Chippewa) legend that was written down by Chief Kah-ge-ga-gah-bowh (George Copway) in the 1850s. It tells the story of an ideal age, when everyone lived forever, healthy and happy. At an appropriate time, spirit messengers would climb down a magic vine linking earth and sky. They would summon venerable members of the tribe to join them in the sky. Spirit messengers could also walk among humans, looking after them and sharing their concerns.

When a certain boy is favored by a spirit messenger, other members of the tribe become jealous and suspicious. They ostracize the boy and taunt him and his grandmother until the boy finally begs the spirit to take him to the sky kingdom. The grandmother's grief causes her to behave rashly, and she climbs the forbidden vine. The vine breaks under her weight, severing the link to the sky kingdom.

After the magic vine is severed, disease and disaster are sent to punish the people of the earth. They no longer will live forever, but will die of illness or old age. To help the people endure the punishment, the gods create the medicine men and reveal to them the secrets of the herbs, flowers, and trees of the earth that can be used for protection, relief, and treatment.

The legend explains the phenomena of disease and death, as it teaches respect for nature and awareness of the environment, its gifts and its power.

Barbara Juster Esbensen is a Minnesota poet who has retold another Ojibwa legend, **The Star Maiden**, and has written several books of poetry for children.

Helen K. Davie's delicate watercolors add considerable depth to the presentation of the legend. Her extensive research into Ojibwa clothing and customs is apparent in her work. The renderings of Ojibwa medicinal plants worked into the borders enhance each illustration.

How do you think the grandmother feels about what she has done? Is she sorry she tried to reach her grandson, or is she sorry she failed? Give reasons for your answers.

Native-American Folk Tales

Words and Pictures

Choose a Native-American legend from **The Sound of Flutes and Other Indian Legends.** Draw a picture to go with the story. You may wish to visit the library to find out about traditional clothing, dwellings, and customs of the Native Americans in the story you have chosen, so that your illustration is authentic. Hang your picture in a classroom exhibit. Include a card that gives the title and short summary of the story.

Season's Greetings

Get together with three other students. The four of you can each write an original legend for each of the following topics:

- Why trees are bare in winter
- Why trees have blossoms in spring
- Why leaves turn color in autumn
- Why leaves are green and fruit ripens in summer

You may wish to brainstorm your ideas with your group and discuss the details for each topic, so that all of the legends go together. Illustrate your legends. Then display your illustrations and have each member of your group read his or her legend to the class.

Ladder from the Sky

Rewrite **Ladder to the Sky** from the point of view of the Sky Messengers. Pretend that you are a Sky Messenger. Explain why you liked the boy so much. Tell how you felt when the boy's grandmother started to climb the sacred vine. Tell what happened when you found out that your link to earth was broken by the boy's grandmother.

The Sound of Flutes and Other Indian Legends
Richard Erdoes
Ladder to the Sky
Barbara Juster Esbensen

To Live in Two Worlds: American Indian Youth Today

By Brent Ashabranner
Photographs by Paul Conklin
Dodd, Mead, 1984

In **To Live in Two Worlds: American Indian Youth Today,** a 1984 ALA Best Book for Young Adults and a 1985 Carter G. Woodson Book Award winner, Ashabranner profiles Native Americans who are struggling to resolve the conflicts and contradictions inherent in trying to bridge two cultures. The need to uphold traditional values is strong in these Native-American youths as they strive to preserve them in their daily lives. At the same time they realize that many educational opportunities are available to them only outside the boundaries of the reservation. Ashabranner interviews a cross section of Native-American youths from a variety of tribal groups nationwide. As their stories unfold, a recurring theme emerges: Education is the key factor that will empower these youths. To obtain it, they must overcome fear, prejudice, loneliness, and the sense of alienation that comes with being separated from home and family. Their hope and motivation to persevere come from the realization that the survival of their people, culture, and heritage depends on their success. Photographs by journalist Paul Conklin accompany the text.

Brent Ashabranner began his career as an English teacher and a prolific writer of stories and articles about the American West. Later, the Peace Corps and other overseas development programs took him to Africa, the Philippines, and Indonesia. His experiences overseas and in the American West contributed to his special interest in writing about Native Americans and American immigrants and refugees. Ashabranner's books for children on these and other subjects have won numerous awards.

Paul Conklin has provided photographs for a number of children's books, including **Cimarron Kid,** and has collaborated with Brent Ashabranner on a number of projects.

What concerns about living outside the reservation were expressed most often by the Native-American youths?

36

When Clay Sings

By Byrd Baylor
Illustrated by Tom Bahti
Scribner's, 1972

In **When Clay Sings,** potsherds serve as a metaphor for history, each piece representing a fragment of time; pieces may be joined by chance or by diligence or by design to present a broader view. Baylor expresses sorrow that the Native Americans' way of life has been lost. But the text also evokes pride in a vital, ongoing heritage and faith in the overriding power of nature. The text is both instructive and imaginative. Baylor reports archaeological facts that uncover evidence of hidden cultures.

Byrd Baylor is the author of numerous award-winning children's books about Southwestern Indian culture. She combines history, lore, philosophy, observation, and wit to build an understanding of tribal life.

Tom Bahti's whimsical renderings of authentic designs mimic the decorative work of the ancient potters of the Southwest.

How is putting together pieces of history like repairing a broken pot?

Arctic Memories

Written and illustrated by Normee Ekoomiak

Henry Holt, 1990

Arctic Memories describes the life-style, culture, and beliefs of the Inuit, a group of tribal nations located throughout the Arctic, including Siberia, Alaska, the Northwest Territories, Arctic Quebec, and Greenland. Through a skillful combination of art and text, Ekoomiak reveals a rich heritage with an underlying purity of spirit that touches every aspect of life. The interplay among Inuit people, animals, and the elements is explained in legend, in historical references, and in narrative captions that are accompanied by original prints, paintings, and needlework.

The range of Ekoomiak's artistic talent and the clarity of his memories combine to give readers a glimpse into the dynamics of an extraordinary group of people whose spirit triumphs over an inhospitable environment.

The text is in Inuit, adapted from the Cree alphabet, and in English.

Normee Ekoomiak was born in northern Quebec and grew up in an Inuit settlement. He studied at the New School of Art in Toronto, where he applied the techniques that were passed down to him from his grandfather. He makes his home in Ottawa, Ontario.

What would be the most difficult part of Inuit life? What would you like most about Inuit life?

The Chinook

By Clifford E. Trafzer

Chelsea House, 1990

The Chinook gives an overview of the history and tragic decline of a civilization of people. Located in the Pacific Northwest along the Pacific coast and along the Columbia River and its tributaries, the Chinook thrived for hundreds of years, fishing, hunting, and trading extensively throughout the region. Meticulously crafted canoes and a special dialect developed for trade enabled the Chinook to dominate commerce for hundreds of miles.

Life for the Chinook changed with the arrival of European and, later, American fur traders and explorers. It is believed that Captain John Meares was the first European to make contact with the Chinook, in 1788. The Chinook were soon hosts to countless captains and crews, trading furs for nails, spikes, cloth, copper, thimbles, and buttons, which they in turn traded with different tribes farther inland. By the end of the eighteenth century, trade between the Chinook and the Europeans was brisk, and the Chinook welcomed the establishment of trading posts and British settlements even though they were puzzled by the newcomers' claims to their lands.

Gradually the Chinook way of life was eroded by the introduction of European influences that undermined the Chinook people's self-reliance. The most notable of these negative influences were firearms and liquor, diseases unwittingly spread by the outsiders, and federal regulations and policies regarding Native Americans.

Trafzer provides information on the Chinook culture, language, crafts, customs, and beliefs, along with a chronicle of their decline over several hundred years, up to and including their present status in recognized and unrecognized groups located on reservations in Washington state. Excerpts from historical records and lexicons, diagrams, and sketches accompany the text, along with etchings, paintings, and photographs.

Clifford Trafzer is a member of the Wyandot Indian tribe and is professor and chairman of American Indian Studies at San Diego State University. He is the author of several books, including a series of children's books about Native Americans.

What about the Pacific Northwest made it desirable to European explorers and traders? How did the Chinook preserve their natural resources?

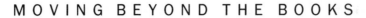

Native-American History/Oral History

Plan for the Future

Pretend that you are a state senator. You would like to be responsive to the needs of the Native Americans in your state. What are some of the problems facing some Native Americans today? On a chart, present a five-year plan showing how you would help the people whom you represent. Explain who and what will be needed to make your ideas work.

A Moment in History

Pretend that you are a Chinook trader meeting European explorers for the first time. Write a story describing your thoughts and feelings. What do you think of the ship captain's clothing and appearance? What interesting things do the sailors have to trade?

Dear Diary

Pretend that you are a European explorer being guided up a river by a group of Native Americans. The journey takes a week. Make up a diary about the trip. Include descriptions of the landscape and your impressions of what you see and learn. What is your camp like? What do you eat? What is the purpose of your trip?

Thoughts of Home

Pretend that you are one of the Native-American students interviewed in **To Live in Two Worlds,** who has been sent far from home to study. Write a letter home. Describe the things that you miss the most when you think of home. Tell your family about the things you are learning and the friends you are making.

The Chinook
Clifford E. Trafzer
To Live in Two Worlds: American Indian Youth Today
Brent Ashabranner

Anpao:
An American Indian Odyssey

By Jamake Highwater
Pictures by Fritz Scholder
Lippincott, 1977

Anpao: An American Indian Odyssey is a Newbery Honor Book recommended for students in upper grades. Anpao, the Dawn, is a young man in search of his destiny. He falls in love with Ko-ko-mik-e-is, who is much sought after by the young men in her tribe. Ko-ko-mik-e-is has refused all suitors because the Sun has claimed her for himself. Anpao must find the Sun and ask for the hand of Ko-ko-mik-e-is, and he must have the Sun remove the scar from his face as a sign that permission is granted. In time it is revealed that the Sun is Anpao's father and that his human mother was destroyed when she tried to return to her people in the World Below.

The Moon, the Sun's wife, is jealous and angry because of her husband's love for Anpao's human mother. She is determined to teach Anpao a lesson as he sets out on his journey. The story of Anpao's arduous quest to find the Sun's lodge and obtain his blessing provides a background for recounting a broad spectrum of Native-American stories and allegories. Notes at the end of the book lend insight into the interwoven stories and the perceptions of reality that they reflect, and also trace the origins of the stories.

Jamake Highwater, whose background is Blackfeet and Cherokee, is the author of **Song from the Earth: American Indian Painting; Ritual of the Wind: American Indian Ceremonies, Music, and Dances;** and **Fodor's Guide to Indian America.** He is an honorary member of the White Buffalo Council, an organization of North American tribal leaders. He holds degrees in cultural anthropology, comparative literature, and music, and he has published extensively in all three fields.

Fritz Scholder is a Luiseno Indian. He is internationally known for his art, which reflects Native-American themes. His lithographs appear throughout **Anpao: An American Indian Odyssey,** and one of his oil paintings is reproduced for the cover art.

If you had been Anpao, when, if at all, would you have been most tempted to give up during the quest?

Iktomi and the Berries: A Plains Indian Story

Retold and illustrated by Paul Goble
Orchard Books, 1989

In **Iktomi and the Berries: A Plains Indian Story,** Iktomi's foolishness gets him into trouble. Iktomi goes hunting laden with all the appropriate accoutrements, but he is inept. He ends up trying to find a way to gather berries from the river, where he sees them reflected in the water, and his efforts are nearly his undoing.

The trickster is a traditional figure in Native-American storytelling. He is known by many names— Iktomi is his Lakota (Sioux) name, meaning Spider. The trickster is sometimes portrayed as a buffoon, and at other times he is shown to be very clever. In some stories, his cleverness is not to be trusted; in others, the trickster's cleverness is put to good use and he is credited with a number of innovations. Generally, however, his behavior exemplifies what *not* to do, providing a lesson that teaches by entertaining.

In the storytelling tradition, Goble uses an interactive style, with prompts for audience reaction and participation woven through the text. In addition, Goble has annotated his illustrations with comments that serve as inside jokes for the reader and may or may not be shared with the audience, as the reader chooses.

Goble's illustrations are richly detailed and bridge the gap between ancestral trickster tales and the mischief that Iktomi is still up to today.

Paul Goble has had a lifelong interest in Native-American cultures. He was born in Haslemere, England, and taught at Ravensbourne College of Art and Design in London. His trips to the United States to study Native-American legend and lore have given him insight into the customs and beliefs held by the various Native-American tribal nations. He has been adopted into the Yakima and Sioux tribes and given the name Akinyan Chikala—Little Thunder—by Chief Edgar Red Cloud.

If you had come upon Iktomi, would you have tried to help him? How?

Ceremony in the Circle of Life

Story by White Deer of Autumn
Illustrations by Daniel San Souci
Raintree, 1983

Nine-year-old Little Turtle is a Native-American boy living in the city, where he is teased, misunderstood, and disappointed by his surroundings. He is confused by the hurt and loneliness he feels; but his cries into the night sky are answered by the Star Spirit from Little Turtle's ancestral past. Star Spirit takes Little Turtle on a journey, pointing out the elements and cycles of the earth and introducing him to the circle of life that connects everything in the universe. The two perform a ceremony that summons the power of the sun to unite the Four Directions so that they may help the people of earth live in harmony with one another and their environment. The ancient traditions the Star Spirit shares comfort Little Turtle because he sees that he is part of the whole and can never be alone.

Delicate watercolors accompany the text, capturing perfectly the dreamlike quality of the story.

Gabriel Horn, who is known as White Deer of Autumn, was named by Princess Red Wing of the Narraganset Tribe–Wampanoag Nation. His uncles taught him the traditional concepts of his people. White Deer served as cultural arts director of the Minneapolis American Indian Center. His poetry has appeared in anthologies and quarterlies. White Deer lives with his family in St. Petersburg, Florida.

A resident of California, Daniel San Souci graduated from the California College of Arts and Crafts. He has illustrated several children's books. **The Legend of Scarface** was chosen as one of the Best Illustrated Children's Books of 1978 by **The New York Times**.

Do you think that Little Turtle ever needed to summon the Star Spirit again? Give reasons for your answer.

Dancing Teepees: Poems of American Indian Youth

Selected by Virginia Driving Hawk Sneve
Art by Stephen Gammell
Holiday House, 1989

Readers will gain insight into Native-American culture through the stark simplicity of style and linguistic precision that characterize the poems in **Dancing Teepees: Poems of American Indian Youth**. Generations of voices are represented in each entry, imparting their history, lessons of life, and hope for the future. The collection includes lullabies, songs, and stories that highlight the phases of childhood from birth to young adulthood. In transcribing these poems from oral tradition, Sneve has preserved the impact and expression of the original spoken words and passes on the essence of ritual, belief, and tradition.

Virginia Driving Hawk Sneve is a teacher, counselor, and antiques dealer. She grew up on the Rosebud Sioux reservation. The poems in this collection were remembered from her childhood or recited to her by others, or they are original works.

Stephen Gammell's artwork, which captures the sweetness and innocence of each poem, reinforces the imagery and represents the content with a sensitivity that all will appreciate.

What did the poems in **Dancing Teepees: Poems of American Indian Youth** *tell you about Native-American family life?*

Native-American Contemporary Fiction

Anpao's Adventures

You and each member of your group can illustrate one of the episodes or scenes from **Anpao: An American Indian Odyssey.** On a large sheet of paper, use paint, chalk, crayons, colored pencils, and colored markers to make your scene come alive. Set up an exhibit of your group's scenes, displaying them in the order that they happen in the story.

All About Iktomi

Write a story featuring Iktomi from **Iktomi and the Berries: A Plains Indian Story.** Put Iktomi in a silly situation and then help him try to find a way out. You may wish to use one of the following three ideas to get you started, or you may come up with an idea of your own.

- Iktomi decides that the easiest way to get honey is to disguise himself as a bear and wait for some bees to come along.
- Iktomi, out hunting, shoots at the sun just as it dips below the horizon and is horrified by the results.
- Iktomi swings across a river on a rope to reach a village that is famous for its canoe builders, and he can't figure out how to get back across when his visit is over.

Illustrate your story and share it with the rest of your class.

Line by Line

Write a poem or a group of poems, using the Native-American themes from your reading. Some ideas include living in harmony with nature, having respect for all living things, or taking care of the earth. For example, you may wish to look at pictures of the Southwest to give you ideas for poems about the mountains and high deserts. Or you may wish to describe the herds of buffalo roaming the prairies a century ago.

Anpao: An American Indian Odyssey
Jamake Highwater
Iktomi and the Berries: A Plains Indian Story
Paul Goble

Exploring Hispanic-American Cultures

In this section, students study the history and demographics of Hispanic cultures to gain an appreciation for their many variations; they compare folk tales from Nicaragua, the Hispanic Southwest, and Mexico; they explore ancient and modern civilizations, focusing on Mexico and Central America, to gain an understanding of historical events and cultural elements influencing the present-day Hispanic-American population; they learn about the lives of youths in Hispanic communities, both in American cities and in Indian villages in Baja and southern Mexico.

Students should appreciate the complex cultural collage making up the Hispanic-American population whose heritage can be traced to Mexico and Central America. In the 1500s, Spanish conquistadores defeated the people of Mexico, marking the end of the extraordinarily advanced civilization created by the Aztecs. Ideas, beliefs, and customs of Indian groups throughout the region combined with European traditions—for example, Indians who converted to Catholicism adopted a form of Christianity imbued with traditional Indian beliefs, ceremonies, and imagery. Also influential were the populations of Moors and Jews in Spain and of Africans who sailed with the Spaniards on their explorations. The Indian cultures and the Spanish colonists' cultures began to come together. Colonists maintained the upper hand, however, relying on Indian laborers to keep the economy thriving as the boundaries of Spanish territory were pushed northward. Franciscan and Jesuit priests supervised the expansion, establishing and populating missions as far north as what is now Nebraska, east to Texas, and west to California. Troubles at home loosened Spain's hold on the colonies in the eighteenth century; in the nineteenth century, *criollos* (people of Spanish descent born in New Spain) and clergy promoted Mexican independence, which was achieved in 1821. Meanwhile, the sparsely populated northern territories were increasingly influenced by American merchants and trappers, who added another element to the cultural mix. American trailblazers became Mexican citizens and married into families of California landowners, and when the Republic of Texas accepted the offer of statehood in 1845, many Mexicans stayed on; the first official Hispanic-American population was established when the U.S. granted citizenship to Mexicans who chose to stay in the new territories after the Mexican War of 1846.

In the Caribbean, the people of Puerto Rico are citizens of the United States. Historically, the island was under Spanish rule, but that country surrendered Puerto Rico to the United States in the 1898 Treaty of Paris. Today, Spanish is the main language taught in the schools, though children are taught English as well. The United States mainland has been strongly influenced by the many achievements of the people of Puerto Rico.

Evidence of the impact of Hispanic-American culture throughout the United States can be seen in music and dance, literary styles and subjects, and cuisines, and is especially apparent in art and architecture. Folk arts including extraordinary handwoven textiles, various forms of pottery, and intricate silverwork have been part of the Hispanic tradition for generations, and some designs and styles are centuries old. With the arrival of the Spaniards, Mexican painters were exposed to European genres and developed entirely new forms that were distinguished by a unique richness of tone and color. In the eighteenth century, sculpture and architecture took precedence over painting, which lapsed in quality until the rise of the Mexican muralists of the early twentieth century. Elements of Italian Renaissance, Moorish, and Gothic design were combined in Mexican decorative arts, particularly wrought-iron work and ornamental architectural detail. The brief reign of Emperor Maximilian fostered the use of French architectural motifs and techniques, and the Craftsman style derived from the California missions still influences architecture, furnishings, and life-style today.

The evolution and redefinition of the Hispanic-American population and the blending of cultures that has been going on for centuries continues today as immigrants and refugees come to settle within America's borders. Many Hispanic-Americans have their roots in Mexico, Central America, South America, the Caribbean, and the West Indies. The majority have their roots in Mexico, Cuba, and Puerto Rico. The rich traditions of all Hispanic-Americans have positively contributed to the cultural life in the United States.

Hispanic Histories

Get together with your group. Choose one of the following Hispanic regions or countries to be your focus for the following activities.

Mexico   Puerto Rico   Cuba   South America
Dominican Republic   Central America

Traditional Togs

Create life-sized paper dolls of a man, a woman, and a child. Draw the dolls in traditional costume from head to toe. Explain the history of the costumes. Explain how they are practical in the native climate and geography, tell how they make use of natural resources, and give any other information you can about how the costumes relate to the family's life-style.

K-TAL TV

Put together a television news program highlighting a major historical turning point in your region. You can highlight an invasion, a natural disaster, a war, the election of a leader, or any important event. Your news program may include an interview with a historical figure, a story by an on-the-street reporter, and an editorial comment.

Pieces of History

Make a bulletin-board display showing the history of your region. Write dates and facts on colorful squares of construction paper. Then put the squares together to create a mosaic showing a typical scene or traditional tile design.

Reporting

Present your research or program to the rest of the class. Discuss similarities and differences between various Hispanic regions.

48

Mother Scorpion Country

Retold by Harriet Rohmer and Dorminster Wilson
Illustrated by Virginia Stearns
Children's Book Press, 1987

Mother Scorpion Country is a Miskito Indian legend from Nicaragua. It is a love story about a young man, Nakili, who cannot bear to be separated from his wife, Kali, when she dies. He journeys with Kali to the land of spirits. When Nakili and Kali reach the spirit world, Mother Scorpion welcomes Kali. She is angered that Nakili is with Kali, but his genuine love earns her sympathy even though she warns him that paradise is closed to him. When Nakili realizes that he does not belong in paradise with Kali, Mother Scorpion returns him to his village, stipulating that he must not tell anyone about Mother Scorpion Country until he is ready to return. Nakili's silence about where he has been makes his family and friends suspicious and frightened of him. Villagers who rejoiced at his return soon shun him. Nakili's resulting loneliness and his longing for Kali convince him to leave the land of the living forever.

Dorminster Wilson, a Jamaican missionary, collected stories of the Miskito Indians in the early 1900s, but his manuscripts were never published. Over the years—especially with the suppression of traditional beliefs and customs by the Somoza dictatorship—stories of Mother Scorpion Country were lost to the culture. In an effort to recapture the Miskito culture, Harriet Rohmer began collecting stories from storytellers and scholars. Wilson's original manuscripts were passed on to her by his grandson. Rohmer's painstaking research resulted in the re-creation of this beautiful tale.

Virginia Stearns's vivid paintings portray the dual perspectives of Nakili and Kali and reinforce the life and death images presented in the story. Since paradise is not open to Nakili, he sees barrenness in the spirit world, while Kali sees brightness and life.

The text is in Spanish and in English.

What do you think Mother Scorpion Country looks like to Nakili when he goes there the second time?

The Invisible Hunters

Retold by Harriet Rohmer, Octavio Chow, and Morris Vidaure
Illustrated by Joe Sam
Children's Book Press, 1987

The Invisible Hunters is a Miskito Indian tale about three brothers from a village on the Coco River in Nicaragua. While hunting wild pig, the brothers come upon an enchanted vine, the Dar, that is able to render them invisible. Immediately the brothers realize the advantage invisibility would give them in hunting wild pig. The vine makes the brothers promise to use its power according to its rules: game must not be sold, and game must not be hunted with guns. The brothers are not in the habit of using guns or selling the meat and so they agree to the terms. Soon the brothers become famous, and word of their hunting ability spreads along the river. Traders come to the village and talk the brothers into selling surplus meat; when the traders' demands outstrip the brothers' supply, the traders give the brothers guns. The brothers reason that the traders must be more clever than the Dar, and all promises are forgotten until one day the brothers return from their hunting to find that they are permanently invisible. Though they beg the Dar to help them, and they beg the elders of the village to forgive them, they are banished forever, and it is said that they still can be heard in the bush, crying "Dar. Dar. Dar."

Working with Miskito Indians, Harriet Rohmer was able to piece together the story. Octavio Chow, a Miskito Catholic clergyman, and Morris Vidaure, who had grown up in a Miskito village, both contributed significant details that Rohmer incorporated into the story. Collages by well-known African-American artist Joe Sam have a whimsical appeal, evoking the foolhardiness of the brothers even before their tragic fate is revealed.

The text is in Spanish and in English.

What might have happened to the brothers if the traders had not heard of their great success?

Cuentos: Tales from the Hispanic Southwest

By José Griego y Maestas and Rudolfo A. Anaya
Museum of New Mexico Press, 1980

Cuentos: Tales from the Hispanic Southwest is a collection of Hispanic stories, tall tales, legends, and myths from New Mexico and southern Colorado, reflecting cultural values. Traditional Indian folklore and medieval European themes—including images of Don Quixote, characters from **A Thousand and One Nights,** and teachings of the Roman Catholic church—are combined and set against the unique backdrop of the Southwest. Because of the geographical isolation of the mountains, canyons, and deserts of the region, which according to Aztec mythology is the sacred place of origin for all of creation, the cultural heritage of the people has been preserved, along with their oral tradition. The stories, which have been written from the original transcriptions collected firsthand by Juan Rael, a Stanford University professor, reflect more than the values, customs, and beliefs of the storytellers. They are also imbued with the heritages of the Moors and Jews in Spain, people of the Philippines, Africans in the Caribbean, and native North and South Americans, whose influences they borrow.

The text is in English and in Spanish, with a glossary of idiomatic words of American or archaic origin.

José Griego y Maestas, who selected and adapted the stories, is a leader in the field of bilingual education and has taught at the College of Santa Fe. He is the director of the Guadalupe Historic Foundation in Santa Fe.

Rudolfo A. Anaya, who retold the stories in English, is the author of **Bless Me, Ultima,** a young adult book that won him national recognition. He teaches creative writing and English literature at the University of New Mexico.

Which of the stories in Cuentos: Tales from the Hispanic Southwest *is your favorite, and why?*

Why Corn is Golden: Stories About Plants

Text adapted by Vivien Blackmore
Illustrated by Susana Martinez-Ostos
Little, Brown, 1984

Why Corn is Golden: Stories About Plants is a collection of ancient Mexican legends about the origins, characteristics, uses, and symbolism of plants found throughout the region. Birds, animals, and insects also play roles in these Indian myths repeated across the countryside. The illustrations by Susana Martinez-Ostos reflect the national stylization and aesthetics established by Mexican artists.

Why do you think people make up stories that give explanations of everyday things?

Hispanic-American Folk Tales

Show and Tell

Choose one of the stories from **Cuentos: Tales from the Hispanic Southwest.** Make a series of pictures that show the story scene by scene. Draw your pictures on large sheets of paper. Practice telling the story you have chosen. You do not need to memorize it word-for-word. If you wish, you may write notes on the back of your pictures to help you. Then use your series of pictures to tell the story to the rest of your class.

Red Hot

Write a folk tale of your own about chilis. You may wish to use one of the following ideas:

- Why are green chilis often hotter than red chilis?
- Why are little tiny chilis often hotter than great big chilis?
- Why are there so many kinds of chilis?
- Tell how chilis got into a soup for the first time and what people thought when they first tasted the soup.

The Power of the Dar

Remembering **The Invisible Hunters,** write a story about some Miskito Indian children who find the Dar plant and use the leaves to make themselves invisible. The Dar warns them not to make any mischief while they are invisible. The Dar tells them to use their power to help the people of their village. What do the children do? Do they follow the Dar's rules, or do they get into the same sort of trouble the hunters got into? If you wish, get together with your group and turn your story into a play. Use simple props and costumes. Perform your play for the rest of the class.

Cuentos: Tales from the Hispanic Southwest
José Griego y Maestas and Rudolfo A. Anaya
Why Corn Is Golden: Stories About Plants
Vivien Blackmore
The Invisible Hunters
Harriet Rohmer, Octavio Chow, and Morris Vidaure

The Maya

By Lawana Hooper Trout
Chelsea House, 1990

The Maya, part of the Indians of North America series, traces Mayan history from ancient times to the present. It begins with the story of creation set down in the Popul Vuh, the Quiche Book of Counsel, which chronicles centuries of sacred and secular history. The Maya today still adhere to the patterns of cosmic order described in the Popul Vuh, striving for harmony between their everyday world and the forces of the cosmos. Trout provides extensive information about the Classic Age of the Maya and the elements that made it one of the most remarkable of ancient civilizations, including sophisticated methods of agriculture and exceptional mathematical and astronomical insight. A detailed explanation of the Maya number system and cyclical fifty-two-year Calendar Round is provided. Photographs and drawings of artifacts and archaeological excavation sites throughout Mesoamerica show temples, palaces, and pyramids and give evidence of intricate trade networks and a thriving economic, spiritual, and political society. As the civilization declined, the Maya became fragmented by civil war and could not unify their efforts to defend themselves against the Spanish conquistadores; but it took the Spaniards twenty years to conquer the Yucatán and nearly two hundred years to bring the Maya of Peten Itzá under Spanish rule. In the centuries following the Spanish conquest, numbers of ladinos (people of Spanish descent) and mestizos (people of Spanish and Indian descent) increased, gradually gaining domination over the Maya. When Mexico won independence from Spain in 1821, the Maya did not gain any rights, and the establishment of Mesoamerican states marked the end of Mayan self-government. Rebellions, uprisings, massacres, and civil strife have comprised Mayan history since then. Supported and encouraged by foreign influences, ladinos continue to control land and commerce. The Maya have had to overcome poverty and deprivation as exploited laborers and as refugees in order to preserve and continue their four-thousand-year-old legacy.

Lawana Hooper Trout teaches English at the University of Central Oklahoma and has edited two high school literature series. She has served as director of summer institutes at the D'Arcy McNickle Center for the History of the American Indian at the Newberry Library in Chicago.

Why is it important to preserve the histories and cultures of ancient civilizations?

Journey Through Mexico

By Barbara Bulmer-Thomas
Troll Associates, 1991

Colorful graphics, charts, maps, drawings, and photographs enhance this region-by-region view of Mexico. The topography, demographics, and principal cultural and social features of each region are highlighted, along with the industrial and/or agricultural economic base. With this informative nonfiction monograph, students gain insight into the colorful variations in the regions that comprise the nation of Mexico.

Barbara Bulmer-Thomas was born in Belize, Mexico's southern neighbor. When she was twelve, her family moved to a town near the Mexican border and she frequently accompanied her father on visits to Mexico. After coming to Britain in 1964, she earned an Open University degree in science and took a postgraduate course in biology at the University of London. She is married to an economist specializing in Latin America, and together they have traveled widely in Mexico and other Latin American countries. At present she is gathering material for a history of British colonies in Central America.

Where in Mexico would you most like to live?
What would you like to do there?

Pyramid of the Sun, Pyramid of the Moon

Written and illustrated by Leonard Everett Fisher
Macmillan, 1988

Pyramid of the Sun, Pyramid of the Moon describes the Toltec settlement that later came to be known by the Aztecs as Teotihuacán, the present site of Mexico City. The story of the pyramids highlights sixteen hundred years of history. Aspects of the Toltec culture are covered: life-style, beliefs, religious practices, and achievements, including the construction of the two sacred pyramids. When the Toltecs lost control of the region and abandoned Teotihuacán, wandering tribes of Chichimecs continued to regard the deserted city as sacred ground. Hundreds of years later, the Aztecs who took over the region were also impressed by the apparent power present in the city and respected the ancient ruins as part of their heritage, incorporating them into their rituals and adding pyramids of their own to the landscape. Fisher eloquently describes and depicts what Cortés saw when he was invited into the city by Montezuma— floating gardens, marketplaces, gold. Fisher also relates Montezuma's betrayal by Cortés and his death at the hands of his own people. Today, the Pyramid of the Sun and the Pyramid of the Moon are all that remain of Teotihuacán, providing a link to the ancient people of Mexico. Fisher's text is accompanied by striking acrylic paintings executed in a primitive style to depict a lost world.

Leonard Everett Fisher has made many notable contributions to children's literature, including **The Great Wall of China** and **Alphabet Art.**

Would you have wanted to visit Teotihuacán in the days before it was destroyed? Why?

Joan Baez

By Hedda Garza
Chelsea House, 1991

Hedda Garza's biography of Joan Baez for the upper grades is not only the story of a talented Mexican-American woman's rise in the music world; it is also a social history chronicling conflict and confrontation throughout the world over the past three decades. There are many victories reported in Baez's story—overcoming prejudice, shyness, and stage fright; struggling to keep what she calls her "demons" at bay; taking charge of her life; realizing her commitment to nonviolence, civil rights, and freedom. Joan Baez's story includes a remarkable array of people in all walks of life all over the globe, both in music circles and in the political arena. The strength of Baez's convictions coupled with her musical gift ensures that her message of peace will continue to be heard.

Hedda Garza has been a free-lance writer for some 25 years. She has written extensively on Hispanic history and politics, and several of her biographies are about famous Hispanics. Her biography **Leon Trotsky** won a New York Public Library award for young adult nonfiction. She has also written biographies of Francisco Franco, Mao Zedong, Salvador Allende, and Pablo Casals.

In what ways does Joan Baez show courage in overcoming difficulties?

Hispanic-American History/Oral History

Visitor's Bureau

Make a travel brochure for a region of Mexico, Central America, South America, the Dominican Republic, Cuba, or Puerto Rico. Describe what a traveler will find special about the area. Include information about the climate, sights, and places to visit. Illustrate your brochure and display it on a bulletin board.

Field Guide to Ancient Times

Pretend that you are an archaeologist. You are studying the ruins of Teotihuacán. Write field notes to describe your work and feelings about the pyramids. What is special about the place? What is it like to work in such an ancient place? How is Teotihuacán still a site of sacred mysteries? Get information from **Pyramid of the Sun, Pyramid of the Moon,** and do your own research as you need to. Have everyone combine their field notes into a notebook to share with the class.

Music of a Lifetime

Choose a selection of recordings or songs sung by Joan Baez, beginning with her work in the 1960s. Combine her music with historical information to create a time line. You may focus on events in Baez's life or on important dates in United States history through the 1960s, 1970s, and 1980s. You may wish to play the music on a record or tape player, learn the songs and sing them yourself or with your group, recite the lyrics without the music, or use all three ideas. Present your "Music of a Lifetime" program to your class. You may wish to invite other classes to share the music. Invite your audience to participate by joining in on some of the songs.

Pyramid of the Sun, Pyramid of the Moon
Leonard Everett Fisher
Joan Baez
Hedda Garza

Family Pictures/ Cuadros de familia

Paintings and stories by Carmen Lomas Garza
As told to Harriet Rohmer
Spanish text by Rosalma Zubizarreta
Children's Book Press, 1990

In **Family Pictures/Cuadros de familia**, an ALA Notable Book, Carmen Lomas Garza reveals memories of a rich and happy childhood in a Texas border town. Family traditions and cultural customs are depicted in detailed paintings; each is accompanied by text in both English and Spanish to explain subjects, settings, and point of view. Students may explore the paintings again and again, finding something new each time. Carmen Lomas Garza has the seasoned artistic skill that comes with years of dedication, and yet her paintings possess a childlike sweetness, wonder, and innocence. She re-creates scenes from her girlhood that show not only the highlights and the humdrum, but also portray the enduring love of her family and strong ties to her heritage.

Carmen Lomas Garza is a renowned artist of many talents. She uses a variety of media in executing her story pictures, including *papel picado*, a traditional Mexican method of cutting paper to create intricate images.

What do the story pictures tell you about Carmen's family? What do they tell you about her Mexican-American heritage?

Baseball in April and Other Stories

By Gary Soto

Harcourt Brace Jovanovich, 1990

Gary Soto's collection of eleven stories for the upper grades are populated by a collection of ordinary Mexican-American youngsters. The stories deal with the problems and uncertainties that all young people face—peer pressure; acceptance; self-consciousness; and the fear, anger, and frustration that accompany these problems. The often rocky transition from childhood to adolescence is a recurrent theme; the difficulties of many of Soto's characters are compounded by poverty and an uncertain future. Family relationships are strained by cultural and generational gaps as children struggle to adjust to the present world, which in many ways differs from that of their parents and grandparents. Soto's characters, however, have great courage, strong family values, limitless determination, and healthy attitudes to see them through. Older students will be able to identify with the characters whom Soto so clearly defines and will appreciate their dilemmas and trials. Some students will gain insight into the cultural dynamics of the Mexican-American family. And many will learn some new ways to cope with the age-old confusion that accompanies growing up. **Baseball in April and Other Stories** is an ALA Best Book for Young Adults, a *Booklist* Editors' Choice, and a *Horn Book* Fanfare Selection.

The text is in English, with some Spanish words. A glossary of Spanish words and phrases is included.

Gary Soto was born and raised in Fresno, California, and now teaches English and Chicano studies at the University of California at Berkeley. His poetry has appeared in many magazines, and in 1985 he received the Before Columbus Foundation's American Book Award for his autobiographical essays.

What do you have in common with the characters in Baseball in April and Other Stories? *Identify one character and tell how the two of you are alike.*

Jaguar, My Twin

By Betty Jean Lifton
Illustrated by Ann Leggett
Atheneum, 1976

Jaguar, My Twin gives students in the upper grades an opportunity to explore a changing culture while they enjoy an engrossing story. Shun is a Zinacantec Indian boy living in a remote village that is at a turning point as the villagers consider the proposed introduction of electricity. Shun's father, a village leader, is in favor of the plan. Others—especially Shun's father's biggest rival, Manvel—are suspicious of government help and see change as a threat. At the same time, Shun himself is at a turning point. As part of his coming of age in the Mayan tradition, Shun's twin spirit has been revealed to him in a dream. His twin is a jaguar, the most beautiful, powerful, and cunning of all creatures. Shun's fate and that of his twin spirit are interconnected; each depends on the other for survival. The strength of this belief is made apparent when Manvel solicits an evil shaman to destroy Shun's father. The shaman is wary of the power that Shun's father's twin spirit might have, so he attacks Shun instead, tricking the gods into forcing the little jaguar out of the safety of the supernatural corral. Shun lies near death as his twin is threatened by the dangers of the wilderness. Shun's family seeks the help of a wise, powerful shaman. She is able to convince the gods to save the jaguar and to punish those who attacked an innocent boy. As Shun recuperates, his dreams provide a glimpse into his own future as a shaman—something for him to think about as he watches the electric lights flickering throughout the village. A wealth of information about religious rites and beliefs, Mayan culture, life-style, food, family relationships, and tribal politics is incorporated into the plot.

Betty Jean Lifton's books include **The Dwarf Pine Tree, The Cock and the Ghost Cat, The Mud Snail Son, The One-Legged Ghost, Goodnight, Orange Monster, Return to Hiroshima,** and **Children of Vietnam.** On a visit to the Zinacantec village, which she later used as the setting of **Jaguar, My Twin,** Lifton was captivated by the people and their culture. Through her research and contact with anthropologists, she met Ann Leggett, the illustrator, who spent several years living with the Zinacantec people.

How might Shun combine his future as a shaman with the knowledge and education he wants to pursue? How is leaving the village like leaving the supernatural corral?

Shark Beneath the Reef

By Jean Craighead George

Harper, 1989

Shark Beneath the Reef offers a unique view of change and conflict in the lives of Tomás Torres, his family, and his friends in Baja, California. Tomás, exploring a reef near his grandfather's fishing camp, glimpses what he supposes is a whale shark. He resolves to catch it, ignoring the warnings that indicate it is a much more dangerous member of the shark family—the hammerhead. The mysterious and menacing presence of the shark is juxtaposed with the ominous threat of the *oficionales* from the Mexican government. The fishermen who have struggled to make a living on the sea for generations are being severely restricted in order to boost tourism. A way of life for Tomás and his family is about to change. At the same time, Tomás faces his own dilemma of whether to continue in school or quit to carry on the family tradition. In addition to a first-rate adventure story, George offers extensive information on Mexican political, cultural, and natural history; marine biology; geography; and contemporary issues.

Jean Craighead George is widely known for her outstanding nature books; **Julie of the Wolves** was awarded the 1973 Newbery Medal.

If you were Tomás, what would your decision about staying in school have been and why?

Hispanic-American Contemporary Fiction

El Gusto Es Mío

Describe a meeting between Tomás from **Shark Beneath the Reef** and Shun from **Jaguar, My Twin.** Both have left their villages to study at the university. Tomás is studying to be a marine biologist. Shun is studying to be a doctor. The two boys meet in one of their classes. Think about why these two boys might become good friends. Think about what they have in common. Then write a dialogue between them when they first meet. Get together with a friend and present your dialogue to the rest of the class.

Story Pictures

In **Family Pictures/Cuadros de familia,** Carmen Lomas Garza celebrates holidays, shares meals, and does other special things with her family. Paint a picture of your own family, extended family, friends, or neighbors. You may be getting ready for a meal or a party or a holiday. You may be out on a Saturday morning doing yard work, washing cars, or just having fun. You may be attending a local event, such as a fair or a parade. Put in as many details as you can that capture what your life is like. Write a story describing your painting and identifying the people you have included. Then display your story and picture on a bulletin board.

Batter Up!

Pretend you are Jesse from "Baseball in April." Winter has gone by, and you are anxious to play ball. Manuel is busy with Little League. You are looking forward to playing for the Hobos. The Red Caps are still in your league, and a few more teams have been added. Write a story about your second season. Or write a newspaper article describing the Fresno Parks League Championship between the Hobos and the Southsiders.

Shark Beneath the Reef
Jean Craighead George
Jaguar, My Twin
Betty Jean Lifton
Family Pictures/Cuadros de familia
Carmen Lomas Garza
Baseball in April and Other Stories
Gary Soto

63

Exploring Asian-American Cultures

In this section, students gain an understanding of the vastness and variety of the Asian continent by exploring the cultural and demographic diversity that is prevalent in that area. This exploration includes finding out about regional crops, cooking, and diet, discovering art forms, and comparing aesthetic styles from one country to another. The literature in this section introduces students to the myths, legends, and fairy tales that reflect the humor, values, and viewpoints of different Asian populations. Students study ethnography, biography, and history to gain insight into the events and circumstances that have shaped people's lives in this part of the world. They are exposed to a wide selection of ideas and information through fiction and nonfiction accounts.

Chinese Americans

Significant immigration of Chinese to the United States began around the middle of the nineteenth century, when news of the Gold Mountain reached Asia from California. At that time, conditions in China had deteriorated, resulting in widespread famine, government corruption, and social unrest. Chinese citizens looking for a means of escape were not allowed to settle overseas, but they could go there to work. A corrupt contract labor system was the only avenue open to workers who could not pay their own passage to the United States.

Although the positive impact the Chinese workers had on the development and prosperity of the American West was immediately apparent, they were met with prejudice and discrimination that increased from decade to decade. Laws were enacted to restrict Chinese workers, deny them access to goods and services, tax their efforts, and outlaw their businesses. The Chinese relied on their considerable ingenuity and determination to overcome these obstacles.

The prevailing anti-Chinese sentiment forced Chinese workers into isolated communities. Chinatowns were established in cities all over the United States. For decades, these Chinatowns were largely comprised of bachelors who were not allowed to travel to China to marry, could not afford to bring family members to America, and were restricted from intermarriage by law. Because the Chinese were not welcome outside their community, they had no motivation to develop language skills or adapt to new customs. Clan affiliations based on last names were established to provide a family structure of support and society that was like village life in China. Traditional celebrations, beliefs, rituals, disciplines, and even styles of dress remained largely unchanged, as did codes and philosophies of Confucianism, Taoism, and Buddhism.

The end of World War II and the gradual repeal of immigration restrictions changed the demographics and character of Chinese-American society. Older members of the Chinese-American population ensure ethnic awareness; younger members bridge cultural gaps and actively seek solutions to problems faced by the Chinese-American community. The rich and extensive legacy of Chinese achievement in art, technology, and science is apparent in all aspects of American society.

Japanese Americans

Except for isolated instances, the Japanese did not come to the United States until the 1880s, almost thirty years after Perry's expedition to reopen trade routes between Japan and the U.S., and a generation after the first influx of Chinese immigrants. Unlike the Chinese immigrant population, which was comprised almost exclusively of laborers, the first Japanese immigrants were students, merchants, sailors, adventurers, and samurai seeking political asylum from the reestablished imperial government. The Japanese were quick to adopt western hairstyles and dress, but in spite of their efforts, they were targets of the same prejudice and discrimination that had prevented the Chinese from joining American society.

In the early 1890s, large numbers of young, single men arrived from Japan to seek their fortunes. Younger Japanese sons could not inherit land and they saw work in America as a means to earn enough to return to Japan and obtain property. Most had no intention of staying in America any longer than necessary. However, the difficulty of saving money, especially with discriminatory hiring policies in full force and anti-Asian sentiments running high, turned a temporary stay into permanent residency that demanded entrance into American life.

As is true throughout Asian cultures, the family is the cornerstone of Japanese society. Perpetuating traditional family roles and interactions proved increasingly difficult as American customs were embraced. Families encouraged children to excel in their studies, hoping that education would be the key to intercultural understanding and tolerance. However, children immersed in the English

language and introduced to American values at school often left Japanese language skills and behaviors behind, impeding communication with family members who did not speak English and were not exposed to the dynamics of American culture.

With the outbreak of World War II, the virulence of anti-Asian sentiment was fully realized. It is important for students to realize that the majority of the Japanese Americans on the West Coast who were detained in work camps were second- or even third-generation American citizens, born and raised in the United States. In some cases, during the evacuation, English-speaking Japanese children were encouraged to assert their independence, either by taking on leadership roles in the newly formed communities or by relocating to midwestern or eastern cities on their own. At the end of the war, regaining lost ground and recapturing old dreams was left largely to the children, who were finally able to realize the goals of their parents.

Japanese immigrants and their Japanese-American children worked hard to recognize and capitalize on the advantages and minimize the disadvantages they encountered in their everyday lives. Japanese aesthetics are characterized by elegant simplicity, formality, refinement, restraint, harmony, grace, energy, and discipline. These qualities, present in all aspects of Japanese culture, have been incorporated into the fabric of American life.

Korean Americans

The Korean peninsula is rich in natural resources, close to Pacific trade routes, and lined with accessible harbors, making it a strategic location and the object of long-time political struggle on the part of China, Japan, Russia, and the United States. Years of conflict resulted in the 1953 creation of two independent Korean nations: The Democratic People's Republic of Korea in the North, and the Republic of Korea in the South. In the years since the end of the Korean War, South Korea has been transformed into a modern and prosperous society with an internationally vital economy, but restrictions on the people's rights as citizens of a democracy have led to widespread dissatisfaction and unrest.

Koreans who immigrated to Hawaii and North America in the early 1900s were met with the same hostilities as other Asian immigrants, and coped in a similar fashion by forming small ethnic enclaves. More recent Korean immigrants have taken an active role in circumventing discrimination by creating their own opportunities. Since many of them could not get desirable jobs, they started their own businesses through an ancient loan system in which a group shares pooled assets—a *kye*. Each person uses the *kye* for a year, retaining the profits and then passing the *kye* on to the next group member. Throughout their 5,000-

year history, Koreans have relied on the characteristic patience, tolerance, and pragmatism that have enabled them to overcome hardships. Here in the United States, Korean Americans have been able to establish and expand business interests and real estate holdings. As with other Asian groups, education has traditionally been crucial to Korean Americans' success, and Korean-American parents encourage their children to achieve academic excellence.

Filipino Americans

The Philippines, a country of islands located on a cultural crossroads, has a colorful legacy and a rich combination of traditions, customs, and beliefs derived from peoples all over the globe. In ancient times, seafaring migrants from Southeast Asia and Indonesia were soon followed by Malays, who were credited with creating the irrigated rice terraces in the mountains of northern Luzon. The Buddhist empire of Sri Vijaya, which had its capital in Sumatra, dominated trade in Southeast Asia for five hundred years; and its influence was present in the Philippines until the Javanese Majapahit empire, with its Hindu influence, came to power in 1293. Philippine trade with China was brisk when the Majapahits took power. Self-governing Chinese colonies were established on the islands from 1372 to 1421 but were eradicated by Arabs who had trade routes through the region. The Arabs brought goods and currency to the Philippines, along with Islam, which was widespread in the islands when Magellan claimed them for Spain in 1521. The Spanish settlers succeeded in uniting the Philippines into a single country that would not gain independence for another 425 years.

In 1896, rebel forces led by Emilio Aguinaldo forced the Spanish government to sign a pact guaranteeing reforms, but the Spanish-American War broke out before the reforms could be implemented. America promised independence to the Philippines in exchange for support in defeating Spain, but when the war was over, the Philippines was ceded to the United States. In 1935, the Philippines became self-governing, though the country remained a territorial possession. During World War II, the Japanese occupied the Philippines; after the Japanese surrendered, the exiled government returned to Manila, and independence was finally granted.

Filipinos joined scouting parties along the West Coast as far back as the late 1500s, and Filipino sailors who jumped ship in North American ports established settlements as early as 1763. The first Filipinos officially admitted to the United States came as students under the *pensionado* scholarship program in 1903. Later, self-supporting Filipino students established "Little Manilas" in cities across the nation, along with social and educational clubs.

In the Immigration Act of 1924, Filipinos were not barred from immigrating as

other Asians were; they were the first American nationals among Asian groups to travel under U.S. passports. California ranchers and Pacific Northwest and Alaskan cannery operators viewed them as a much-needed labor source. Filipinos were, however, subject to the same strong prejudice aimed at other Asian groups. Laws in the western states severely restricted or prohibited their movements. Filipino doctors, lawyers, teachers, and other professionals could not get licensed to practice in the West and moved to the Midwest or the East.

Although Filipinos could not enjoy all the freedoms of democracy, they fought hard to preserve them during World War II. Filipino-American volunteers were instrumental in liberating the Philippines. Their loyalty and patriotism changed American attitudes, so that laws prohibiting property ownership, restricting citizenship, and preventing interracial marriage were repealed when the war was over.

Today, Filipino Americans are the fastest-growing Asian group in the United States. Like members of the other Asian groups who have come to America, Filipino Americans believe that success hinges on education and hard work, and their commitment to achieving their goals reflects these beliefs.

Southeast Asian Americans

Southeast Asian culture has been influenced by the countries that have controlled the region over the centuries. China ruled Vietnam for hundreds of years; the Portuguese established trade routes and business ventures in the region and introduced Christianity; Dutch traders set up commercial centers in the north, followed by the English and the French, who established colonial rule that lasted until the Japanese occupation of World War II. Laos has been influenced by its Thai heritage, Khmer domination, and French rule. Cambodia's Khmer civilization was greatly influenced by Indian Hindu traditions—as evidenced by artistic and literary styles—and later was influenced by French rule. Thailand escaped European colonialization, though France and Great Britain exerted great pressure, as did Japan.

Over the centuries, all of the countries in the region have been subjected to civil war, strife, and national and international conflict. The effects have been devastating, and many people in the region have looked to the United States for freedom, asylum, and peace.

In their efforts to reach America, the Southeast Asian refugees have overcome separation from family and homeland, survived weeks at sea, and endured months to years in crowded relocation camps. They are well equipped with the motivation and determination required to meet the challenges of adjusting to American life.

Asian River Trip

The Mekong River is one of the greatest rivers in the world. It begins in the Tibetan highlands of China. There it is called the Dza Chu. It flows south out of the mountains, forming swift rapids and rushing through deep gorges. It forms the border between Laos and Myanmar. It flows through northwest Laos and forms part of the border between Laos and Thailand. From there it flows onto the Cambodian plain, where it is joined by the Tonle Sab during the dry season. The Mekong flows into the South China Sea in a delta that covers part of Cambodia and Vietnam.

Get together with your group. Choose one of the countries of the Mekong River to be your focus for the following activities.

River Resources

How does your focus country depend on the waters of the Mekong River? Possibilities include drinking water, food, transportation, hydroelectric power, irrigation.

River Ports

Pinpoint cities located along the river in your focus country and research them. You may also wish to explore some of the main tributaries of the Mekong that flow through the country.

River Flow

If your focus country is Cambodia, describe the relationship among the Mekong, the Tonle Sap, and the Tonle Sab. How does this relationship change during the year?

Reporting

Get together with the rest of the class for a Mekong River trip. Provide maps for your presentation, so that you can point out the highlights on your leg of the trip.

The Rainbow People

By Laurence Yep

Illustrated by David Wiesner

Harper, 1989

The Rainbow People is a collection of Chinese tales translated and retold. They were chosen because of their link to America, the land of the Golden Mountains; all were originally collected in the 1930s in Chinatown in Oakland, California, though they are primarily set in China and deal with traditional subjects. Editorial notes introduce each section and shed light on recurring themes. Trickster tales caution listeners to keep their wits. Fables about why things are the way they are, found worldwide, focus on predestination and the perceived inability of an individual to change the world. Tales about fools deal with misinterpretations, misunderstandings, mistakes, and common human failings, along with bad luck and dangers of the unknown. Tales of virtue and vice reveal the rewards of acts of kindness and the perils of greed, pride, hubris, and jealousy. Tales from America recognize the strain of coping in a new environment under difficult circumstances. Tales of love describe devotion that overcomes time and distance, keeping alive dreams of home and the hope of reuniting with loved ones left behind.

Laurence Yep was born and grew up in San Francisco. His novel **Dragonwings** was chosen ALA Notable Children's Book of 1975 and 1976 Newbery Honor Book, and was given IRA's 1976 Children's Book Award. Yep is the author of numerous other books for children about Chinese people. He teaches creative writing at the University of California at Berkeley.

How might sharing folk tales from home help immigrants adjust to life in a new place?

70

The Two Foolish Cats

By Yoshiko Uchida

Illustrated by Margot Zemach

Margaret K. McElderry Books, 1987

Yoshiko Uchida's **The Two Foolish Cats** is a reworked version of a traditional Japanese folk tale. In it, two cats possess opposite traits that may inspire teamwork or tension, depending on the cats' moods and their circumstances. The two cats get to squabbling over the division of rice cakes and are persuaded by the badger to take their problem to the wise old monkey of the mountain. The monkey settles the argument in a way that is satisfying only to him. Although his solution is disconcerting to the cats, it delights the forest denizens who have to put up with them.

Yoshiko Uchida grew up in northern California and is the author of twenty-five books for children and adults, many of which have won awards.

Margot Zemach is a Caldecott winner who is noted for her illustrations of her own work and of other authors' work. Her watercolors for **The Two Foolish Cats** have the delicacy and detail of Japanese paintings, yet still show the fur-flying frivolity of the cats' antics, the humor of the badger, the caginess of the monkey, and the glee of the forest creatures.

Do you think that Big Daizo and Little Suki will go to the badger for advice or go to the old monkey for help ever again? Explain your answer.

The Chinese Mirror

Adapted by Mirra Ginsburg
Illustrated by Margot Zemach
Gulliver Books, 1988

This whimsical, lighthearted story tells of a Korean man who travels to China and brings back with him a tiny mirror as a souvenir. The powers of the mirror delight him, for when he looks into the shining object, a merry face is hiding there. The man's wife becomes curious about his glee, but when she looks at the mirror, she is dismayed to discover that her husband has brought home a beautiful young woman. Her mother-in-law insists that the object holds an elderly lady; her father-in-law sees only an old man. When the man's young son peeks at the object, he discovers a boy who has taken his toy. A neighbor who comes to comfort the little boy claims he sees a bully who makes little children cry. The neighbor promptly shatters the mirror, thereby getting rid of *all* the inhabitants of the mirror and the problems they caused.

Mirra Ginsburg is a translator, anthologist, and editor who has also written many children's books. Several of her books, including **How the Sun was Brought Back to the Sky** and **Good Morning, Chick**, have been translated for a worldwide audience. She lives and works in New York City.

Margot Zemach, a noted author and illustrator, studied the work of Korean genre painters Sin Yun-bok and Kim Hong-do in order to re-create authentic images in the eighteenth-century style. Zemach lives in Berkeley, California.

What might have happened in the story if two people had peered into the mirror at the same time?

Rockabye Crocodile

By Jose Aruego and Ariane Dewey
Greenwillow, 1988

In this traditional Philippine tale, Amabel and Nettie are two grandmotherly boars with distinct personalities. Amabel, the cheery boar, sets out to go fishing. Her song attracts the attention of a bamboo tree that rains minnows into her basket. Amabel continues on her way, and when she comes upon a mother crocodile with a crying baby, she cares for the baby and is rewarded by its mother with a basket of fish. When Nettie hears of the story of Amabel's day, she can't wait to try it herself. However, the bamboo tree is not so receptive to Nettie's brusque demands and rough treatment, and the baby crocodile is inconsolable in Nettie's cursory care. When Nettie gets home with the sealed basket that is her baby-sitter's fee from the angry mother crocodile, she is horrified to discover that it is filled with spiders, scorpions, rats, and bats. Amabel arrives just in time to whisk the creatures out the door. Nettie is duly ashamed of herself and vows to improve her attitude and soften her approach. As a result, the boars arrange to take turns caring for the baby, and the mother crocodile happily supplies them with fish.

Jose Aruego and Ariane Dewey are a well-known team of illustrators. They have over three dozen books to their credit, including the ALA Notable Book **We Hide, You Seek**, which they also coauthored.

Do you think Amabel was surprised to hear of Nettie's unfortunate experiences? Do all people have days when they feel and act like Nettie even though they try to be like Amabel?

The Brocaded Slipper and Other Vietnamese Tales

By Lynette Dyer Vuong

Illustrated by Vo-Dinh Mai

Lippincott, 1982

The Brocaded Slipper and Other Vietnamese Tales is a collection of traditional Vietnamese fairy tales. Students will find familiar elements—such as a frog prince, Thumbelina, wicked stepsisters, fairy kingdoms, broken spells, princesses disguised as servants—in intriguing new settings. Characters' predicaments are also familiar, though Vietnamese fairy enchantment does not always guarantee a happily-ever-after outcome.

Lynette Dyer Vuong collected folklore and fairy tales during her thirteen-year stay in Vietnam. She adapted the tales in **The Brocaded Slipper and Other Vietnamese Tales** from original Vietnamese texts.

Vo-Dinh Mai was born in Hue, Vietnam, and studied art there and in France. Over the past three decades, his paintings have been exhibited all over the world, and he has illustrated many books. He lives in Maryland with his family.

What parts of the Vietnamese fairy tales remind you of fairy tales you know from other parts of the world? What parts are special or different from other fairy tales?

Cambodian Folk Stories from the Gatiloke

Retold by Muriel Paskin Carrison

From a translation by The Venerable Kong Chhean

Charles E. Tuttle, 1987

This collection of folk tales reflects the ancient Cambodian oral tradition of explanatory tales, fanciful tales, entertaining jokes and riddles, and lessons. The folk tales of the *Gatiloke*, which means "the right way for people of the world to live," were sermons given by Buddhist monks. Most of the stories are about ordinary people stymied by ordinary dilemmas, with special emphasis on the virtues of prudence, moderation, and foresight. The book is divided into parts: scoundrels and rascals, kings and lords, and foolishness and fun. Each story is followed by an editorial note to clarify the imagery and the outcome, providing further insight into Cambodian culture, beliefs, and values. An appendix provides a historical overview and maps, and a glossary and a reading list are also included.

Muriel Paskin Carrison met Dr. Kong through her work with Cambodian refugees in Southern California, where she is a professor of education at California State University, Dominguez Hills.

The Venerable Kong Chhean was born in Compong Cham Province, Cambodia, and was ordained a Buddhist monk in 1956. He studied in Cambodia and in India. Since 1979, he has worked with Cambodian refugees in Southern California, promoting understanding of the culture and heritage of Cambodian Americans as they adjust to a new world.

How do the stories from the Gatiloke show that people are rewarded for taking time to use their heads?

Beyond the East Wind

Told by Duong Van Quyen
Written by Jewell Reinhart Coburn
Illustrated by Nena Grigorian Ullberg
Burn, Hart, and Company, 1976

The stories in **Beyond the East Wind** trace the mythological history of Vietnam, beginning with the first royal family headed by the Dragon ruler, Lac Long Quan, and Au Co, the Fairy Queen. The mythical Hung Vuong dynasty spans eighteen generations, from 2879 to 259 B.C.; Hung Vuong 17 and Hung Vuong 18 appear in several of the tales that chronicle the end of that era. Legends provide information about philosophical, spiritual, and social conventions, including women's roles, animism, Confucianism, family values, and codes of behavior. Some stories incorporate Vietnamese words, which are translated in the extensive notes at the end of the book. A short history of Vietnam is also included. Stories are illustrated with pencil drawings that combine authentic Vietnamese motifs with traditional themes.

Jewell Reinhart Coburn has lived, worked, and traveled extensively in the Far East and has studied Asian cultures. Her association with Southeast Asians began when she volunteered to help refugees at Camp Pendleton near her California home. Collaboration on her books has grown out of her friendships. Titles include **Khmers, Tigers and Talismans: From the History and Legends of Mysterious Cambodia** and **Encircled Kingdom: Legends and Folktales of Laos.**

How might ancient legends of victorious heroes have inspired Vietnamese people in their modern-day conflicts and efforts to achieve independence?

Asian-American Folk Tales

Two Foolish Cats II?

Write another episode for **The Two Foolish Cats.** Use the book to remind you of the cats' personalities and physical appearance. If you wish, include the badger and the monkey in your story. Try to illustrate your story using a Japanese style or technique. Share your story with the rest of your group. You may wish to put all of the stories into a book entitled **More "Two Foolish Cats" Tales** for your classroom or school library.

What's New?

Write a folk tale similar to **The Chinese Mirror.** Create a story about what happens when someone finds an unfamiliar object, such as a pair of sunglasses or binoculars, and shows it to the people in the village. Or you may wish to describe what happens when a child hears thunder for the first time and goes through the village getting different explanations for the source of the sound.

A Fantastic Tale

Choose a favorite character from a Vietnamese folk tale. You might select a character from one of the stories in **The Brocaded Slipper and Other Vietnamese Tales,** or a mythical figure from **Beyond the East Wind.** Write your own fantastic tale featuring that character. Your story can be a sequel or something entirely new. Think about the adventures and surroundings the character had in the original folk tale, and what the character is like.

What a Boar!

Write a story featuring crabby Nettie and sweet Amabel from **Rockabye Crocodile.** You may wish to describe something that happens while they are taking care of the baby crocodile. Write and illustrate your story in the form of a comic book, and display the pages on a bulletin board.

The Two Foolish Cats Yoshiko Uchida	**The Brocaded Slipper** **and Other Vietnamese Tales** Lynette Dyer Vuong	**Beyond the East Wind** Duong Van Quyen
The Chinese Mirror Mirra Ginsburg		**Rockabye Crocodile** Jose Aruego and Ariane Dewey

Traditional Asian Foods

What can you find out by studying what people eat? You may be surprised to know that a family dinner can tell you about the climate, geography, history, religion, and customs of a region or country.

Get together with your group. Choose one of the Asian countries listed below, or any other Asian country you may be interested in, as a focus for the project.

China	Japan	The Philippines	Korea
Vietnam	Laos	Cambodia	Thailand

Find out about traditional foods served in your focus country. Make up a menu. Describe each dish, including its ingredients, how it is prepared, and any other information. Have fun designing your menu on a large sheet of construction paper. You may wish to use the written language of your focus country on part of the menu.

- If China is your focus country, compare cooking ingredients and styles found in different regions of the country. Explain reasons for the differences. You may wish to make up separate menus or present the information on separate pages or sides of the same menu.
- If Japan is your focus country, describe the country's dependence on the sea for food. Also explain how the need to import foods influences diet and cooking.
- If Korea is your focus country, describe how kimchi is made and how it is served.
- If the Philippines is your focus country, explain how Chinese and Spanish colonial rule influenced diet and cooking.
- If a Southeast Asian country is your focus, describe how French colonial rule influenced diet and cooking.
- If Thailand is your focus country, describe how Malaysia and the Muslim population in the south influence diet and cooking.

Reporting

Present your menu to the class. Explain your findings and describe a typical meal—both what kinds of foods are served and how the meal is conducted. Display the menus on a bulletin board.

Journey Through China

By Philip Steele
Troll Associates, 1991

Journey Through China introduces students to the vast regions and diverse demographic groups that make up the Chinese population. The journey begins in Beijing. Photographs include Tiananmen Gate and the Forbidden City, a Children's Day parade, and part of the Great Wall. To the north, the grasslands of Inner Mongolia are home to descendants of the tribe of Genghis Khan; to the northwest lies a rugged wasteland inhabited by Islamic groups whose language is related to Turkish; to the south is the isolated Buddhist region of Tibet and the Himalayas. In the forested Sichuan province, the rivers flow out of the mountains into the Chang Jiang (Yangtze), the world's third longest river; the river is busy with commercial and commuter traffic connecting the villages, towns, and cities, including Chongqing and Shanghai. The Yunnan province is characterized by a temperate climate, rich farmland, and picturesque countryside that stretches to the tropical forests of the Myanmar frontier. The Zhujiang waterway flows through Yunnan and Guangdong to the port city of Guangzhou (Canton) on the South China Sea, a major industrial center. Coal, steel, and the traditional porcelain made from white clay are produced in the Jiangxi province, which is linked to Beijing by way of the Grand Canal. Hong Kong and Taiwan are also described, along with an overview of customs, festivals, and holidays. A Fact File at the end of the book provides information about language, geography, demographics, the calendar, religion, industry, and agriculture, and also includes a time line of Chinese history from ancient times to the present.

Philip Steele has worked in children's book publishing since 1971 as an editor and writer, and has written many books for children on the natural world and on social history. His extensive overseas travels have resulted in a number of atlases for young people and books that describe life in foreign countries. China is one of the countries he has visited. He lives in North Wales.

What further information about living in China would you like to have?

Commodore Perry in the Land of the Shogun

by Rhoda Blumberg

Lothrop, Lee & Shepard, 1985

In 1853, Commodore Matthew C. Perry anchored his fleet in Edo Bay near Shimoda, Japan, with a letter for the emperor from President Millard Fillmore. President Fillmore hoped to convince the Japanese people to open their ports and establish trade routes between Japan and North America because the United States needed coal and provisions for its whalers. Since Japan had not allowed anyone but a handful of Chinese and Dutch traders into its waters in over two hundred years, the proposal was bound to be sensitive, and diplomacy was of the utmost importance. Blumberg gives a lively, two-sided account of impressions, assumptions, demands, and negotiations, providing a fly-on-the-wall view of both positions. At the same time, she offers a fascinating look at the rigid feudal system that was in effect in nineteenth-century Japan. To enhance and highlight information in the text, appendixes and notes are provided. Among them are a transcript of the Japanese response to President Fillmore's letter, lists of gifts given and received on both sides, and a transcript of the treaty. The text is accompanied by Japanese woodblocks from original handbills, illustrations from scrolls, and reproductions of Japanese art, along with drawings made by the official artists of the Perry expedition.

Rhoda Blumberg is a researcher and writer whose topics reflect her boundless curiosity and imagination. She is the author of **The Truth About Dragons, The First Travel Guide to the Moon,** and **The First Travel Guide to the Bottom of the Sea**, which was chosen 1983 Children's Book of the Year by the Child Study Association.

What would you have thought if you had been one of the first Japanese people to see the tall ships of Commodore Perry come chugging into the harbor?

Children of the World: South Korea

Edited by Sally Tolan, Mary Lee Knowlton, and Mark J. Sachner
Photography by Makoto Kubota
Gareth Stevens, 1987

This book profiles eleven-year-old Bae Jyung Ho, whose family lives in Seoul, South Korea. The photographs offer an insider's view of Jyung Ho's home, his family life, and his school; life in the city of Seoul, including traditional and modern features; and South Korean holidays and festivals. Students may be intrigued to discover that Jyung Ho's routine, school subjects, and activities are similar to their own, though the photographs reveal a world that is very different in style and appearance. Included is a visit to Jyung Ho's cousins, who live in a farmhouse in Chunchon, northeast of Seoul near the 38th parallel. The 1950–1953 war had a great impact on this region of the country, and after the war, Chunchon was rebuilt and made more modern.

A section at the end of the book provides information about South Korean history, demographics, religion, government, language, culture, education, industry and resources, physical geography, and economy. The section also includes a discussion of South Koreans in America, a glossary, and suggested projects and activities.

Compare your life to Jyung Ho's. What are the similarities? What are the differences?

The Filipinos in America

By Frank H. Winter
Lerner Publications, 1988

The Filipinos in America begins with an introduction to the Philippines, its history, and its people from ancient times to the present, through Spanish rule, annexation to America, World War II, and the granting of independence and self-rule. Following this introduction is a discussion of the history of Filipino settlement in America, from the 1500s to the present.

Filipino sailors crewed aboard Spanish galleons exploring the California coast in the late sixteenth century; settlements were well established by the late eighteenth century, and many sailors chose a new life in the New World. The first confirmed Filipino immigrants to the United States jumped ship in New Orleans in 1763 and established a settlement there. The first official Filipino immigrants were students who came to study on government scholarships through a program authorized in 1903. Documentation of the exploitation and restriction of Filipino immigrants through the twentieth century is given, along with accounts of Filipino Americans' extraordinary loyalty and dedication to the United States, and their tolerance of an intolerant society. The last chapter in the book highlights contributions and accomplishments of individual Filipino Americans in art, entertainment, music, medicine, education, and other fields. Photographs accompany the text.

Frank Winter is an assistant curator in the Space Science and Exploration Department at the Smithsonian Institution. His interest in and exploration of the Philippines and its people is a lifelong avocation that is supported by his Filipino wife.

How do you think Filipino immigrants in the 1920s felt about democracy when they arrived in the United States and experienced it firsthand?

Thailand

By Sylvia McNair
Childrens Press, 1987

This volume in the Enchantment of the World series gives a comprehensive history of Thailand, devoting chapters to geography, Bangkok, history, religion, agriculture and industry, everyday life, arts and entertainment, and future projections. The rich diversity of Thai culture is exemplified in numerous detailed color photographs, which are especially effective because of the large format of the book.

Sylvia McNair, the daughter of Methodist missionaries, was born in Korea. She is the author of numerous travel books and articles and is active in professional organizations for publishers and writers in the Chicago area.

If you were planning a trip to Thailand today, what would you be most interested in seeing, and why?

Prince Sihanouk

By Madhavi Kuckreja
Chelsea House, 1990

Prince Sihanouk, a volume in the World Leaders Past and Present series, tells of Sihanouk's rise to power, beginning in 1941 with his role as adolescent puppet king. Under his leadership, postwar independence from French rule was finally achieved. Determined to put his shrewd political abilities to work, Sihanouk abdicated in 1955 in order to run for the office of prime minister. Throughout the 1960s, Sihanouk struggled to keep Cambodia neutral in the face of Communist influences and attacks in neighboring countries, allowing Communist forces to maintain supply bases in the country and accepting aid from the West, including the U.S. and France. A right-wing coup led by Sihanouk's premier forced him into exile in 1970; he set up a government-in-exile in Beijing. Kuckreja provides clear and concise background information about Cambodia's demographics, religious groups, geographical features, and diplomatic, cultural, and political ties to other nations. Sihanouk's life story embodies the political history of Cambodia in a period of considerable upheaval, controversy, tragedy, turmoil, and unrest. This story is unfinished, both for the prince himself and for the Cambodian people.

Madhavi Kuckreja holds a master's degree in political science from the New School for Social Research in New York City. She has worked at the United Nations and at the National Lawyers Guild. She is currently working for a human rights and relations organization in New Delhi.

How did Sihanouk's desire to remain neutral bring about his downfall?

Laos

By Ralph Zickgraf
Chelsea House, 1991

This volume is part of the Places and Peoples of the World series. It offers a geographic, historical, political, social, and cultural view of Laos, a landlocked country that has for centuries been subject to the whims and strategies of outsiders. Laos is a lush country of tropical rain forests. It is home to a variety of indigenous groups and has only a fledgling national identity.

Primarily black-and-white photographs accompany the text. There is a separate section of color photographs. A glossary is included.

__What group of people in Laos would you most like to visit and get to know? What about this group interests you?__

Asian-American History/Oral History

In-depth Interviews

Choose a region, city, or village from an Asian country. Find out about the people's lives there, either in the past or in the present. Gather details about education, family life, celebrations and festivals, and work. Choose the role of a person living in your region, city, or village. Use the details you have learned to create a personality, with experiences, family ties, and plans.

Work with a partner. You and your partner will role-play two different Asian immigrants. Tell your partner your name, your age, the year, where you emigrated from, where you live, who the members of your family are, what your day is like, and so on. Have your partner tell you about his or her Asian persona. Then you and your partner can use each other's information and descriptions to introduce each other to the class.

You may wish to add to your story by describing how your life changed when you moved to America, what you miss about your homeland, how the new community you live in compares with the community you are from, and other comparisons between your new life and your life in your homeland.

Continue until all partners have introduced each other.

Asian Art Forms

Get together with your group. Choose one of the Asian countries listed below, or any other that you are interested in, as a focus for the activities.

China	Japan	The Philippines	Korea
Vietnam	Laos	Cambodia	Thailand

Made By Hand

People of all cultures express themselves through art. Clothing, baskets, pots and dishes, household furnishings, and other everyday things are handcrafted with skill and beauty. These practical items have artistic value, too. Find out about a traditional handicraft or art form. Describe its products and their uses. Create an example of your own or show pictures of authentic works. Possibilities include basketry; calligraphy and printing; painting; sculpture; carving; metalwork; pottery and porcelain; woodworking, including lacquer work; weaving, fabric painting, and other textile arts; paper making; and paper folding. Individual members of your group may wish to focus on one or more art forms, so that collectively your group covers several art forms.

Make Merry

Find out how people celebrate special events or holidays in your focus country. Music and dance are important parts of any celebration. Describe traditional musical instruments and how they are used. Find out about national theaters or dance groups that perform folk dances or ballet. If possible, learn a traditional song or folk dance that you can teach to the rest of the class.

Reporting

Get together with the other groups and share your art forms. Describe and display handcrafted items. Sing traditional songs, perform dances, or describe or put on theatrical productions.

Tales from Gold Mountain

By Paul Yee
Paintings by Simon Ng
Macmillan, 1990

Paul Yee has combined his knowledge of history, culture, and folklore to create eight original stories of the Chinese in North America. The stories are written in the spirit of folklore and legend but depict life in a new, sometimes frightening, and often unfriendly place. Yet the outcome of each story reflects the optimism, good humor, hope, and diligence exemplified by the Chinese people in their determination to find a home in a hostile environment. Each gives the reader a unique view of Chinese history and tradition, as well as insight into the Chinese people's ingenuity in overcoming the obstacles of western culture.

Paul Yee, a third-generation Chinese-Canadian, grew up in Vancouver's Chinatown. He is the author of several children's books and a history of the Chinese in Vancouver. He is multicultural coordinator for the Archives of Ontario.

Simon Ng's paintings capture the drama, loneliness, love, strength, ruthlessness, and pathos of Yee's characters. The style of each painting has a haunting quality, evoking the mystery hidden in each story. Ng was born in Brunei and immigrated to Canada in 1971. He holds several design and illustration awards.

What do the stories in **Tales from Gold Mountain** *tell you about the importance of family relationships even when the family members are separated by time and distance?*

In the Year of the Boar and Jackie Robinson

By Bette Bao Lord
Illustrations by Marc Simont
Harper, 1984

The story of Shirley Temple Wong starts at the beginning of the year of the Boar (1947). Shirley and her mother are about to journey to the United States to join her father, who has found a job and an apartment in Brooklyn. When Shirley reaches America, the overwhelming array of new things that she must get used to and understand are described in a month-by-month account. Most upsetting for Shirley is her loneliness as she struggles to fit in with her classmates. Shirley relies on the wise teachings of her Chinese heritage to give her patience and strength, and she is determined to find her niche. The Brooklyn Dodgers capture Shirley's imagination, and the enthusiasm she shares for the home team and its star player, Jackie Robinson, earn her a place in the group. Baseball is used as a metaphor for the spirit of America, a place where individuals have the opportunity to make a difference. The mounting tension of the pennant race carries this story's action along. **In the Year of the Boar and Jackie Robinson** is a study in hope. It marks a year filled with changes, setbacks, and milestones and anticipates a year of triumphs—including a winning season.

Bette Bao Lord draws on her own experiences as a Chinese immigrant to tell Shirley's story. She is the author of the bestselling **Spring Moon**, a novel for adults that was nominated for the American Book Award for a First Novel, and of **Eighth Moon**, a novel for adults that describes her sister's life in China.

Marc Simont's illustrations gracefully depict the many faces introduced in the story. He is well known for his illustration of children's literature and he received the Caldecott Medal for **A Tree is Nice** by Janice May Udry.

What did you most admire about Shirley Temple Wong? What do you think was the most difficult part of her adjustment to American life?

The Sign of the Chrysanthemum

By Katherine Paterson
Illustrations by Peter Landa
Crowell, 1973

Students in the upper grades will enjoy this story about Muna ("No Name"), a young boy living in medieval Japan. When his mother dies, Muna resolves to locate his father, reputed to be a great samurai warrior, whom he will know by the tattoo of a chrysanthemum on his shoulder. Muna stows away to get to Kyoto, a city of warring clans, corruption, and poverty. Over and over, Muna is faced with difficult choices and tempted by evil forces. His decisions are often unsound; but in the end, he succeeds by finding something he did not realize he was seeking—himself.

Katherine Paterson was born in China to missionary parents and grew up in China and the United States. As an adult, she did missionary work of her own in Japan. She has received much recognition for her work, which has been published internationally. Award-winning titles include **The Master Puppeteer,** winner of the 1977 National Book Award; **Bridge to Terabithia,** winner of the 1978 Newbery Medal; **The Great Gilly Hopkins,** a Newbery Honor Book and winner of the 1979 National Book Award; **Jacob Have I Loved,** winner of the 1981 Newbery Medal; and **Come Sing, Jimmy Jo,** an ALA Notable Book.

What does Fukuji, the swordsmith, see in Muna?

Aekyung's Dream

Written, illustrated, and translated by Min Paek

Children's Book Press, 1978; revised 1988

Aekyung is a Korean girl, newly arrived in the United States. In her loneliness and isolation, even the songs of birds sound alien to her. At school she struggles with language barriers, stereotypes, and discrimination—her classmates tease her about being "Chinese," different, a foreigner. Aekyung keeps her misery to herself; she does not want to upset her parents, who are working hard to make a life for the family in a new place. Every morning, Aekyung dreads going to school and facing the other students.

A visit from Aekyung's aunt, recently returned from a trip to Korea, sparks Aekyung's imagination. She dreams of King Sejong, a revered fifteenth-century Yi Dynasty ruler. His words give Aekyung the strength she needs to meet the challenges of adjusting to life in America. Little by little, she learns to communicate with her classmates and is able to assert herself in her new environment. Aekyung is able to share her Korean background and heritage with others, and she and her new friends gain understanding, tolerance, and appreciation of one another's individuality.

The text is given in both English and Korean. English-proficient students may gain a sense of what Aekyung's bewildering school experience was like if they cover the English words and puzzle over the Korean words and pictures; students who are acquiring English will identify with Aekyung. Others will gain valuable insight into how people from other cultures feel and how they would like to be treated.

Min Paek immigrated to the United States from Korea in 1973. She has worked as a professional artist in both countries. She has also worked as a family counselor at the Korean Community Service Center in San Francisco.

If Aekyung were a new student in your class, what would you and your classmates do to make her feel welcome?

The Little Weaver of Thai-Yen Village

Written in Vietnamese by Tran-Khanh-Tuyet
Translated by Christopher Jenkins and Tran-Khanh-Tuyet
Children's Book Press, 1977; revised 1987

Hien is a young girl living in a Vietnamese village, who manages to maintain a lighthearted sweetness even though her life as well as her way of life is constantly threatened by war. Hien is weaving a blanket for her soldier father, but is interrupted to take rice to a nearby village that has been leveled by the war. When she returns home to her grandmother and mother, she is hustled into a shelter as bombings begin. Her home is hit, her family is killed, and Hien is badly hurt.

In the hospital Hien is frightened and alone, unable to speak because of her injuries. She dreams of the spirit bird, Me-Linh, long a symbol of courage and strength for her people in time of war. Hien is comforted by the image of the bird and is determined to be brave. When she is told that she must go to the United States for medical care, she is afraid, but realizes that her survival and that of her people depend on her journey; when she becomes strong again, she must return to help her people.

Once in the U.S., Hien is cared for by a family that sees her through her surgery and recuperation. She appreciates their kindness but is homesick and lonely and thinks only of her faraway village. Gradually Hien is able to express her feelings about her country and share its history and her experiences with others. Hien's American family gives her a loom, so that she can resume her weaving. Hien makes blankets to send to Vietnam; woven into the design of each blanket is the spirit bird, Hien's link to her people and her heritage.

Tran-Khanh-Tuyet adapted **The Little Weaver of Thai-Yen Village** from a true story of one of the many Vietnamese war-injured children brought to the San Fransisco Bay area for medical treatment. It embodies the plight of the refugees, uprooted by tragedy but sustained by their courage and strong link to their homeland.

How does Hien continue to gain strength from Me-Linh the spirit bird?

The Land I Lost

By Huynh Quang Nhuong
Pictures by Vo-Dinh Mai
Harper, 1982

The Land I Lost gives students an insider's view of life in a Vietnamese hamlet. Huynh Quang Nhuong tells of his childhood adventures and his family, neighbors, and friends. His friends include birds and beasts as well as people. Most students will find the stories and events remarkable, though it is clear that the people living in the hamlet are accustomed to training baby otters to fish for them, having a water buffalo in the family, or living with the considerable threats of wild hogs, horse snakes, and crocodiles. **The Land I Lost** provides many insights into Vietnamese life, including engaging accounts of family history, local customs, traditional beliefs, and daily routines.

Huynh Quang Nhuong was born in Mytho, Vietnam. After earning a degree in chemistry from Saigon University, he was drafted into the South Vietnamese army. Battle wounds left him permanently paralyzed, and he came to the United States for medical treatment in 1969. Since then, he has earned bachelor's and master's degrees in French and comparative literature from Long Island University and the University of Missouri. Huynh lives in Columbia, Missouri. This book is an autobiographical account of his childhood.

What did you find most remarkable about Huynh Quang Nhuong's childhood experiences?

My Best Friend, Duc Tran

By Dianne MacMillan and Dorothy Freeman
Pictures by Mary Jane Begin
Julian Messner, 1987

My Best Friend, Duc Tran opens with the meeting of two boys, both new arrivals to an apartment complex in Southern California. Duc Tran and his family are from Vietnam. Eddie, the narrator of the story, and his family are from Kansas City. The two boys become fast friends, and Eddie learns about Vietnamese customs and culture as he gets to know Duc's family. Family dynamics and values are shown in the relationships of Duc with his sister, brother, sister-in-law, grandmother, parents, nephew, and a family friend. They all live, study, and work together in the family-owned restaurant; Vietnamese celebrations and holidays are explored; Vietnamese foods are described in detail, both at the dining table and at the Vietnamese market.

Dianne MacMillan has a teaching background but now devotes all of her time to writing children's books and raising her family. Dorothy Freeman is also an educator and has written over twenty books. She currently writes and evaluates bilingual education projects in Southern California.

What did you learn about Vietnamese family life from reading My Best Friend, Duc Tran?

Asian-American Contemporary Fiction

Muna's Monologue

Think about the character Muna from **The Sign of the Chrysanthemum.** Pretend that you are Muna as an old, old man. You are known throughout Japan as a swordsmith. Write a monologue telling about your life and how Fukuji trained you in his art. Tell about all of the things he taught you. Present your monologue to the rest of the class.

Gold Mountain Matinee

Get together with your group. Choose one of the stories in **Tales from Gold Mountain** and turn it into a play. Write out stage directions and speaking parts. Decide on simple props and costumes you will need. You may wish to paint a mural on butcher paper for a backdrop to set the scene. Perform your play for your class, your parents, or other students in your school.

My Best Friend Eddie

Remembering the characters in **My Best Friend, Duc Tran,** write a story about Duc Tran and Eddie from Duc Tran's point of view. Describe something the boys do together, such as go on a camping trip, visit a science museum, or go to a baseball game. What does Duc Tran think of Eddie and his family? Does he like what they eat? Does he like their home and the way they live? What does he think of the experiences he is having in his new country? If you wish, illustrate your story before you share it with the rest of the class.

Made by Hand

Use a large sheet of construction paper to make a blanket like those woven by the title character in **The Little Weaver of Thai-Yen Village.** You may use paint, crayons, colored pencils, and markers. Include in your design the image of the spirit bird, Me-Linh. Hang your blanket in the classroom for everyone to enjoy.

The Sign of the Chrysanthemum
Katherine Paterson
Tales from Gold Mountain
Paul Yee

My Best Friend, Duc Tran
Dianne MacMillan and Dorothy Freeman
The Little Weaver of Thai-Yen Village
Tran-Khanh-Tuyet

Further References

For Students

In addition to other works by the authors whose books have been highlighted here, the following resources are recommended for students.

Troll Associates   Titles in the following series:
> *Native American Biographies, Easy Biographies, First-Start Biographies, Journey Around the World, Native American Legends*
> Cassettes and videos on multicultural subjects are also available.

Chelsea House   Titles in the following series:
> *Black Americans of Achievement, Hispanics of Achievement, Indians of North America, Peoples of North America, Women of Achievement, World Leaders Past and Present*

Children's Book Press   Titles and materials on a wide range of multicultural topics

Childrens Press   Titles in the *Enchantment of the World* series

Gareth Stevens   Titles in the *Children of the World* series

Lerner Publications   Titles in the *Visual Geography* series

Silver Burdett   Titles in *Alvin Josephy's Biography Series of American Indians*

Many titles selected for the PBS series *Reading Rainbow* have multicultural themes and are highly recommended for students.

Folklore and fairy tales from around the world are located in the 398.2 section of the library.

For the Teacher

Books about trends in multicultural education often contain comprehensive book lists, projects, activities, and teaching tips. The following titles are highly recommended.

Banks, James A. and Banks, Cherry A., eds. *Multicultural Education: Issues and Perspectives.* Allyn and Bacon, 1989.

_____. *Multiethnic Education: Theory and Practice.* Second edition. Allyn and Bacon, 1988.

_____. *Teaching Strategies for Ethnic Studies.* Fifth edition. Allyn and Bacon, 1991.

Cech, Maureen. *Globalchild: Multicultural Resources for Young Children.* Addison-Wesley, 1991.

Norton, Donna E. *Through the Eyes of a Child: An Introduction to Children's Literature.* Third edition. Macmillan, 1991. Contains an excellent chapter about multicultural literature for children.

Tiedt, Pamela, and Tiedt, Iris. *Multicultural Teaching: A Handbook of Activities, Information and Resources.* Third edition. Allyn and Bacon, 1989.